As Long as We Are Not Alone

Dear Barbara &
Nick —
with love
for all these
years!

Leah

[Hebrew script]

As Long as We Are Not Alone

Selected Poems

ISRAEL EMIOT

*A bilingual edition in Yiddish and English,
translated and with introductions and notes by*

LEAH ZAZULYER

Tiger Bark Press * Rochester, NY * 2015

Published by Tiger Bark Press,
202 Mildorf Ave., Rochester, NY 14609.

Designed by Philip Memmer.

Cover art from a print of the original artwork by Richard A. Beale, 1970.

ISBN-13: 978-0-9860445-5-7

In Memoriam

Brina Menachovsky Rose,
my Canadian partner in the literal translations.

Boris Kaminker,
my Russian refugee surrogate grandfather.

Jim Watson,
my partner in life.

Contents

Preface

AMERICAN POET THEODORE ROETHKE once reminded himself in a notebook that the ultimate struggle in our time was against soul sickness. Israel Emiot, born the year after Roethke in a much less fortunate place, was afflicted, became one of our ultimate exiles, a survivor who did not survive even as he survived. As Holocaust "survivor" Angie Suss Paull once said, even those "who will live will die." From his early 20s, much as he tried to convince himself that he was alive, much as there were sometimes momentary assuagements for him by way of music and in nature, the enduring man felt that his "wandering soul" was like "a mother with her dead child in her arms."

The vacancy and lostness in *As Long As We Are Not Alone* are stunning, and almost unrelieved. Emiot's tone, as translator Leah Zazulyer says, is "somber and bereft." In a lifetime of poems, "the rooster has ceased to wake," melody has a "haunting gnaw," flowers are withered even while in bloom, his heart is "alienated and remote," his "dispirited shadow rests" between life and death, memorial grounds are "soaked with the anguish of children's souls," a "lament-filled past" bursts from every stone like cries from a strangled throat," "the clouds carry a black corpse," he feels the destruction of the Temples *in him,* he is the keeper of a cemetery that is himself, he feels inside him "only the tears of empty corridors," he would like to divorce himself. And on, and on. At the end of the world, his vision tells him, when people have "nothing better to do,/they will slit each other's throat, and die."

There is so much fear and existential dread here in Israel Emiot's life's work in poetry that, in the end, the only thing I can find comfort in during such heavy reading is his courage as he clings to a faithful non-faith that it is *poetry* alone that might make him feel, for at least the duration of the poem, not alone. Amen.

William Heyen

Introduction

ISRAEL EMIOT WAS BORN in Ostrov-Mazoviecka, near Warsaw, in 1909, and died in Rochester, New York, in 1978. Although raised in his very orthodox maternal grandparents' home, his own widely read father had left Poland when Emiot was nine for the USA to become a doctor, but died a year or so later. Emiot wrote a quantity of poetry, but also short fiction, criticism, and later a Gulag memoir. Yiddish was his native as well as his writing language. Numerous books, articles and poems were published in Poland, and one in Russia, during his early life, which coincided with one of the times of a great flowering of Yiddish literature and poetry in particular.

His peripatetic life was emblematic of Jewish writers in the twentieth century. After a very religious upbringing geared toward his becoming a rabbi, and an arranged marriage, he gravitated to the distinguished, "enlightened," and more secular Warsaw Literary Circle, "Tlomatka 13." In 1939, he fled to Bialystok in Soviet Russia when the Germans invaded Poland at the start of World War II. There followed a typical required work battalion in Kazakhstan, a period in Moscow, and a subsequent assignment as a journalist in Birobidjhan. The latter was followed by seven years of a ten year sentence in a Stalin era hard labor camp during a time of renewed Soviet atrocities against Jews. After his release he eventually returned to Poland for rehabilitation, and then spent his last twenty years in the USA, where the wife and two children he had lost track of during the war now lived.

In Rochester, he produced some of his most lyrical if alienated poetry, edited a tri-lingual journal, *Jewish Roots,* and served as a writer in residence at the local Jewish Community Center, despite ill health. He also spent time retrieving or re-writing his poetry which was lost or misplaced during his war and Gulag times. He was at work on a mostly new collection at the time of his death.

His poetry includes sonnets, historical monologues, triolets, and very contemporary free verse. It contains a variety of themes: of landscape, tradition, nostalgia, family, current events, love, and alienation. Emiot maintained contact with other important Yiddish writers world-wide, and participated in the far-flung modernization movements in Yiddish literature. The name

Emiot was a pseudonym. He was also known earlier by his paternal and/or maternal last names: Yanofsky, and Goldwasser.

Section I

1932–1936

Poland

From Alone with Oneself, Drop in the Ocean, *and* At My Side

THE BOOKS FROM WHICH THESE POEMS WERE TAKEN were all published in Poland during Emiot's twenties. These were preceded by some earlier poems published in an orthodox journal, newspaper, or anthology, sometimes in Hebrew. They represent Emiot's earliest attempts to venture beyond writing that complied with the strictures of his particularly religious, Chassidic upbringing, which basically disapproved of "secular" poetry. If one had concerns in life one was supposed to pray to God. No doubt the poems included herein, were influenced by his association for a period of time with the members and evolving modernist philosophy of the Warsaw Literary Circle, called Tlomatka 13—named after a street address. Many of its members became distinguished writers, and then extinguished writers during the Stalin era or World War II. He was also influenced by his absent father's hidden books.

His first book, *Alone with Oneself,* consisted of twenty-two triolets. The triolet was first noted in the thirteenth century. In fifteenth century France it was popular as a vehicle for charming, playful, humorous, amorous, or emotionally distanced verse. Later they were written in Ireland. It is a strict form comprised of eight lines in two stanzas. The second and eighth lines are the same, and a tight rhyme scheme is employed. Usually the triolet pivoted on an uninterrupted transition between the fourth and fifth lines, in order to produce something of a dizzying effect.

Emiot was apparently drawn to this form because of its seemingly emotionally remote circularity and quasi-mystical and/or religious world view. But his triolets create an almost entirely new genre with real substance, evident pathos, ample use of nature, and over-arching anguish. They are, in the best sense of the word, profoundly philosophical and inherently questioning. Throughout his literary career he continued to return briefly to the form—more and more expansively; indeed his triolets changed the tone of the form then and brought it forth into contemporary poetry. It is interesting to note that musical metaphors are conspicuous by their absence in his triolets. Only one, number XXI, uses an extended metaphor for the self—a taut guitar which has lost its chords.

In *Drop in the Ocean,* Emiot wrote two long ballads about Odl Kookanish. They are tales of an actual historical figure in Lemberg during the

Middle Ages. Surely Emiot had read the major Jewish writer I.L. Peretz's version of the same incident in his story "Three Gifts." Nor was Peretz the only writer who used the incident. However, Emiot's retelling is more attuned to the socio-political implications of the event, to the inherent anti-Semitism of Odl's tragic end, and to Jewish-Christian relationships during the Middle Ages. While Emiot keeps Peretz's emphasis on her piety and modesty, he injects an ironic and even sarcastic quality, by contrasting her purity to the evil society around her. (Some think Peretz would have approved of this.) Emiot's long poem in two parts uses a rhymed couplet form to emphasize the tight, closed, finality of the tragedy. Yet he manages to convey her inner state of mind as well. After the lengthy poems about Odl, in a poem titled "Still Landscape," Emiot uses his knowledge of the biblical story of Jacob to bridge the gap between earth's hazards and "heavenly mirth." This book also includes a poem called "Summer," which contrasts the brevity of a butterflies' life span with the seemingly boundless joys of summer, and uses his earliest metaphor about the musical sounds in nature. It is no accident that this poem follows close upon the agony of Odl's long and cruel public death, and that the innocence of nature is contrasted with the evils of mankind.

In *At My Side*, Emiot diversifies both his form and content, free at last to fully explore his own poetic voice. In "The Children's Room," which is addressed to a small child, Emiot touchingly acknowledges the vulnerability of childhood, but reassures the child that all will be well by personifying the heavenly bodies on the one hand, and the toys on the other. It is essentially a domestic poem by an adoring parent, but then followed by a triolet that blames himself, the "soul's caprice," for the difficulties encountered in life. However, the poem "Hour of All Hours," is a rhymed, fourteen-line, complex cosmology replete with thwarted love, vanishing human emotions in the universe, a belief in the existence of the soul "unbound from the body," and his pent up, "everlasting" desire. It is interesting to contrast the universe described in the two preceding poems with this one. Clearly Emiot had been reading his beloved Rilke's Book of Hours before writing this poem. It is a young man's poem, perhaps his most intricate love poem, and one that is aware of the sonnet form. (At some point it was translated into German and anthologized. It is also one of his early poems that he brings forward into his final working book manuscript, and does so without changing a word.) A short untitled poem, rich in metaphor, expresses a more despairing adult view of the universe. A long, far-ranging poem called "My Father," follows without rhyme. Set on the final day of Passover, it is actually his father's life story told in very personal terms. Thus it is his first real poem of mourning, a poem that maintains a remarkable balance between loss and love, pride and resentment: "all America can't /substitute for a small glass of ceremonial wine."

Belatedly, I discovered that a long fatalistic poem, called "Everlasting," was also included in this book. My comments about it are to be found in the Section II, *Siberia*, where Emiot chose to place it without its original title.

Alas, one can only speculate about what might have been the strengths of the final but lost book from this period of Emiot's life, *Over Partitions*.

דער ווייטיק ליגט אין האַרץ — אַ בר־מינן אין הויז
און גראָד איז שבת הײַנט מען טאָר נישט קלאָגן...
אַבֿלים זיצן שטום שווער דעם צער צו טראָגן
דער ווייטיק ליגט אין האַרץ ווי אַ בר־מינן אין הויז...

איז דאָפּלט גרויס דער צער דאָס אומגליק דאָפּלט גרויס
פֿאַרן מויל נישט אויסגעדאַכט טיף אין האַרץ טוט נאָגן...
דער ווייטיק ליגט אין האַרץ — אַ בר־מינן אין הויז
און גראָד איז שבת הײַנט: מען טאָר נישט קלאָגן...

II

Pain lies in the heart—a corpse left in the house,
and now it's Sabbath and one must not moan...
Mourners suffer silently their burdensome sorrow's groan
as pain lies in their hearts like dead bodies in a house...

Doubly great are grief and sorrow when mouths
can't voice that which gnaws deep where the heart's alone...
Pain lies in the heart—a corpse left in a house
as now it is the Sabbath: one mustn't moan...

אויף פֿעלדער דאָס האַרבסטיקע שוויגן
דערמאָנט אין דײַן נאָענטקײט מײַן ג——ט!
און שטיל־שטיל פֿאַרנעם איך דײַן סוד
אויף פֿעלדער פֿון האַבסטיקן שוויגן.

און גרינג איז דער זעל יעצט צו שטײַגן
צום הימל פֿון זינדיקער שטאָט.
אויף פֿעלדער דאָס האַרבסטיקע שוויגן
דערמאָנט אין דײַן נאָענטקײט מײַן ג——ט!

III

The autumnal silence of the fields
reminds me of your nearness, God;
quietly, quietly I absorb your secret
from the silence of the fields

where it's easy for the soul to yield—
to rise above the sinful city's sod
in the autumnal silence of the fields
remembering the nearness of God!

זאָג אַ ברודער וואָס קווייילט און פלאָגט דעם יונגן טייך?:
כוואַליעס לויפֿן און שלאָגן קאָפּ אין ברעג,
ווי מענטשן וואָס האָבן פֿאַרלוירן זייער וועג...
זאָג אַ ברודער וואָס קווייילט און פלאָגט דעם יונגן טייך?...

מיט שפֿע רונד אַרום איז זומערס ברכה רייך
מיט גאָלד באַלאָדן קייטלען זיך די טעג
זאָג אַ ברודער וואָס קווייילט און פלאָגט דעם יונגן טייך
כוואַליעס לויפֿן און שלאָגן קאָפּ אין ברעג

VII

Brother tell me what torments and tortures this little river
whose waves rush to bash their heads on the shore
like people who have hope no more...
brother tell me what tortures and torments the little river

around which abundant blessings of summer quiver
laden with days linked like golden ore—
brother tell me what torments and tortures this little river
whose waves rush to bash their heads on the shore.

ס׳האָט דאָס פֿישעלע אַ זונענשטראַל אין וואַסערס טיף
דערבליקט, און אויפֿגעשוווּמען מיט פֿרייד דער זון אַנטקעגן
און די וועענטקע נישט דערפֿילט וואָס וואַרט אויף ברעגן
פֿאַרן פֿישעלע ווי אַ זונענשטראַל אין וואַסערס טיף.

ס׳איז אַ מעשׂהלע וואָס באַגלייט אונדזער לעבנס שיף
אונדזער לעבן לאַנג אויף אַלע זײַנע וועגן:
ס׳האָט דאָס פֿישעלע אַ זונענשטראַל אין וואַסערס טיף
דערבליקט, און אויפֿגעשוווּמען מיט פֿרייד דער זון אַנטקעגן

VIII

A small goldfish—ray of sun in deep water,
caught sight of the real sun and joyfully swam up to meet it
not anticipating the bank's fish line waiting to greet it—
that little fish like a ray of sunlight in deep water.

It was a small happenstance but it taught her
how the whole ship of life can easily turn to defeat,
yes a small golden fish—a ray in deep water
saw the sun and joyfully swam up to meet it.

ווייסטו צו וועם כ׳וואָלט דיך געגליכן בלאַנדזשענדיק אַצינד
אויף וועגן הינטערשטאָטישע בײַ דער שקיעה רויט?
צו אַ מוטער מיטן קינד אירס אין די אָרעמס טויט,
וואָלט איך דיך געגליכן זאָל מײַנע בלאַנדזשענדיק אַצינד

און טראָגסט דאָס לעבן ווי אַ מוטער דאָס טויטע קינד
וואָס קען זיך דערמיט נישט שיידן... די טרײַסט אין איר נויט...
אָט צו וואָס כ׳וואָלט דיך געגליכן בלאַנדזשענדיק אַצינד
אויף וועגן הינטערשטאָטישע בײַ דער שקיעה רויט...

IX

Know what I'd compare you to now my wandering soul?
To streets on the shtetl's outskirts as distant as the sunset,
to a mother with her dead child in her arms, I regret
I would now compare my wandering soul,

you, carrying your life like a mother in woe
who can't part with the small comfort of her dead child yet,
that's what I'd compare you to now, wandering soul—
to streets as distant as the red sunset.

אַ האַרץ — צי קענסטו אין דער ריי באַפֿעלן מאַרשירן?
און ווען עס קאַרטשעט זיך פֿאַר לייד
מיט מאַסן גיין, פֿאַרמישט מיט זייער פֿרייד,
אַ האַרץ — צי קענסטו אין דער ריי באַפֿעלן מאַרשירן?...

אַ האַרץ — צי קענסטו וועגן מיט אַ ליניע ווירען?
אַ מאָל זידט אַ קראַטער דאָרט, אַ מאָל אַ שטיל געבעט...
אָ האַרץ — צי קענסטו אין דער ריי באַפֿעלן מאַרשירן
ווען עס קאַרטשעט זיך פֿאַר לייד...

XV

A heart—can you order it to march in a line
when it contorts in pain,
order it to walk jumbled together with joy just the same,
can you order a heart to march in a line?

A heart—can you lay out its path with a straight edge every time
if a violent volcano or quiescent crater are not the same?
Can you order a heart to toe the line
when it's crumpling in pain?

וואָס קען איך באָבע מער פֿון דיר פֿאַרלאַנגען
מער ווי דײַן זיפֿץ און דײַן שטילן טרער
אויף מײַן גורל וואָס ביטער איז און שווער
וואָס קען איך באָבע מער פֿון דיר פֿאַרלאַנגען?...

און אויף די אַלע נישט־געטרייסטע באַנגען
און אויף דער נשמה מײַנערס נאָענטסטן באַגער
וואָס קען איך באָבע מער פֿון דיר פֿאַרלאַנגען
מער ווי דײַן זיפֿץ און דײַן שטילן טרער...

XVI

What more can I ask, grandmother
than your sigh and your tears
at my fate so bitter and wearisome,
what more can I ask grandmother

for all this inconsolable remorse, these other
dearest yearnings of my soul... I fear
I cannot ask of you more grandmother
than your sigh and your tears.

מיד פֿון טאָגגערויש כ׳זיץ אין פֿעלד אַליין,
פֿון ווײַטן פֿון שטאָט ברענגט אויף פֿליגל אַ ווינטל
האַלב טויטן געטומל און געשרייען אַ בינטל...
מיד פֿון טאָגגערויש כ׳זיץ אין פֿעלד אַליין.

ס׳איז שטיל אַזוי אין פֿעלד קעגנסט הערן דאָס געוויין
פֿון דער זעל אויף טיפֿע האַרצנס גרונטן...
מיד פֿון טאָגגערויש כ׳זיץ אין פֿעלד אַליין
פֿון ווײַטן פֿון שטאָט טראָגט זיך אויף פֿליגל אַ ווינטל.

XVIII

Tired of the day's tumult, I sit alone in a field
far from the city... but the wind sends me on its wings
half dead noises, shouts and such things—
Tired of the day's tumult I sit alone in a field

so quiet it yields the crying of the soul—
from deep in the heart it sings...
Tired of the day's tumult, I sit alone in this field
far from the city, but the wind sends me things on its wings.

זע: די וועלט איז ערשט אַ גיטאַרע מיט סטרונעס אָנגעצויגן...
אָט פֿאַלן אַקאָרדן שטיל זאָל אַ ווינטל געבן זיי אַ וויג...
און דו ביסט אויך אַן אַקאָרד פֿון דער פֿאַרבלאָנדזשעטער מוזיק
וואָס ציט פֿון וועלט אַצינד ווי אַ גיטאַרע אָנגעצויגן...

און בליבסט אַזוי אַליין...באַלד טוט דער טאָג זיך נויגן
אַ פֿאַרבלאָנדזשעטער אַקאָרד וואָס קען דעם וועג נישט טרעפֿן צוריק
זע, די וועלט איז ערשט אַ גיטאַרע מיט סטרונעס אָנגעצויגן
אָט פֿאַלן אַקאָרדן שטיל זאָל אַ ווינטל געבן זיי אַ וויג...

XXI

See now the world is a guitar from whose strings
chords float forth like a swing wafting in wind;
you too are such a chord, a lost-its-way musical thing
drawn from the world's taut guitar strings

and so you remain alone...'til day plays and sings
a chord that has lost its way-back-wings;
see now the world is a guitar from whose strings
chords float forth like a swing wafting in wind.

אַזוי פֿיל רחמים ברודער טריפֿט ערשט לאַנגזאַם פֿון די הימלען נידער...
וואָלסט געשוווירן: ס'האָט דער פֿאַרנאַכט זײַנע אָדערן אויפֿגעשניטן ברייט,
זײַן בלוט צו צאַפֿן אין קינדער אויסגעבלייכטע צעוואַלגערט איבער גאַסן
אַזוי פֿיל רחמים ברודער טריפֿט ערשט לאַנגזאַם פֿון די הימלען נידער...

און ווי פֿאַרן מענטשנס צער וואָלטן ביימער ערשט געהויבן זײַערע גלידער
מיט צוויגן ווי די הענט אויפֿגעהויבענע פֿאַרגאַן אין אַ שטיל געבעט...
אַזוי פֿיל רחמים ברודער טריפֿט ערשט לאַנגזאַם פֿון די הימלען נידער...
וואָלסט געשוווירן: ס'האָט דער פֿאַרנאַכט זײַנע אָדערן אויפֿגעשניטן ברייט...

XXII

Brother, so much mercy drips slowly down from the skies
you would swear evening had slashed its main veins
and bled on pale children scattering streets and plains nearby;
brother so much mercy drips slowly down from the skies

out of pity for people the trees lift their limbs on high,
their branch arms raised in silent protest and pain;
brother so much mercy drips slowly down from the skies
you would swear evening had slashed its veins.

די באַלאַדע פון דער קדושה
אָדל קיקעניש.

א.

— וואָס איז עס דער "רינגפּלאַץ" אין לעמבערג דער שטאָט
אַ פּולער פֿון יובל נישט צו שטעלן קיין טראַט
די פֿענער עס פֿלאַטערן איבער די הײזער,
דאַרף זיך דער קעניג אַצינדערט באַװײזן?
— קיין קעניג געקומען, דאָך גרויסעס פּאַסירט
די יודישקע אָדל װערט צום שײטער געפֿירט,
אויפֿן שײטער אין פֿלאַמען צו װערן פֿאַרברענט
איז נאָך װי`ניק פֿאַר דעם װאָס האָט מיט אײיגענע הענט,
אַ קריסטקינד דערמאָרדעט צו זײגן דאָס בלוט,
אויף מצות צו נוצן װי באַװוסט עס איז גוט,
עס איז שוין אַדורך אַפֿילו דורכן סאַנד,
ס`האָט די יודישקע אָדל נישט לייקענען געקאָנט
עס איז אויך דער אורטייל געװאָרן געהערט:
די פּיס איר צובינדן צו אַ װיידל פֿון פֿערד,
און אַזוי־אַ דעם פֿערד איבער גאַסן צו טרײַבן
טאָ װער קען זשע אַצינדער אין שטוב איבערבלײַבן,
און נישט זען װי ס`קומט אָפּ פֿאַר איר זינד,
אַ יודישקע דערצו נאָך אַ קצינס אַ קינד,
דעם קצינס אַ טאָקטער און אַלײן אויך גאָר רײַך
די חוצפּה פֿון יודן האָט גאָרנישט קיין גלײַך
די זאַלצגרובענס אַלע אין דראָהאָביטש אין פּאַקט
געהאַלטן, און אַ הויז זיך געװיעט אין פּראַכט,
אָט אַזוי־אַ זאָל אָפּקומען די טאָפֿלטע שטראָף
נאָך אַ פֿערד זיך נאָכשלעפֿן און אויפֿן פֿיער צום סוף
די יודישע טאָקטער װאָס האָט געװאַגט און באַגערט
צום פֿרייַק זיך גלײַכן אויף פּוילישער ערד.

The Ballad of Odl

Odl A

Why is the Ringplatz in the city of Lemberg
so crowded you can't take another step
and flags flutter above the houses—
as though there's a Jubilee?
Will the king now have to make an appearance?
—No king came; nevertheless, important things happened:
The Jewish woman Odl is led to the pyre
to be burned by flames.
It's little enough, for with her own hands,
she murdered a Christian child,
and as everybody knows Jews do,
she sucked out its blood to make matzos!
Her crime's already been processed by the Judicial Court,
so Odl the Jew has had no chance to deny it,
besides, the verdict's already been heard:
Her leg is to be tied to the tail of a horse
and the horse in this manner driven over the streets.
So then, who would remain at home and not watch
this Jewish woman, child of a leader,
daughter of a Cohen, moreover independently wealthy,
atone for her sins?
After all, the nerve of Jews has no equal;
it is they who lease and control the Dorohbts salt mines,
and built themselves a magnificent home.
Thus the double punishment shall be carried out:
This Jewish daughter will be pulled after a horse,
and ultimately set on fire,
this Jewish daughter who dares to covet equality
with a landowner of Polish soil!

ב.

דער רינגפּלאַץ אין לעמבערג שאַלט שוין פֿאַר פֿרייד,
ס׳איז דער שטיטער אין פֿלאַמען צום ברענען שוין גרייט
קיין שפּילקע צו שטעקן אין מענטשן־געדראַנג
מען שטייט שוין אויף דעכער, דער מאַרק איז פֿול שוין פֿון לאַנג
אין מיטן דעם רינגפּלאַץ פֿאַרן ראָטהויז
איז אַ טיש אויסגעשטעלט פֿאַרן ריכטער לענג אויס
דאָרט זיצן די ריכטער אין סויבלנע היטלען
אין רויטע און לאַנגע סאַמעטענע קיטלען
דער טיש איז געדעקט מיט אַ בלאָ טוך מיט טראָאַלדן
דער אורטייל איז גרייט שוין אָט ווערט ער געמאָאַלדן
אין אַ זײַט שטייט דאָס פֿערד, אַ ווילד פֿערד און וואַרט
צום ווײַדל געבונדן צו שלעפּן אויף דער ערד
אָדל בת משה וואָס אין אַ זײַט שטייט פֿאַרטרערט
פֿון טאָרטורן און פּײַנען אין תּפֿיסה פֿאַרצערט
אַ רגע איז מפֿסיק אַ גלאָקן־געקלאַנג,
דער בישאָף צו אָדלען: וואָס איז דײַן פֿאַרלאַנג
— וואָס איז דײַן פֿאַרלאַנג יודישע טאָכטער אַ זאָג
אין מינוט אין דער לעצטער פֿון דײַן לעצטן טאָג,
האָסטו אַ וווּנטש אָדער אַ ווילן
אַחוץ דײַן לעבן מיר וועלן אַלץ דערפֿילן.

Odl B

The Ringplatz in Lemberg resounds with joy.
The pyre's flames are ready to employ.
The crowd's so thick you couldn't stick in a pin;
people stand on roofs; the marketplace's long been packed for
        this sin.
In the middle of the Ringplatz in front of the city council's
        dwelling
a table has been placed lengthwise for the judges to do their
        thing.
There sit the judges in sable hats,
and long red velvet robes; all that's
at a table covered with a blue tasseled cloth.
The judgement is ready; it will soon be announced
        to the harassed Odl.
At the side stands a waiting horse—a wild horse
to be tied by the tail of course
to Odl the daughter of Moyshe, who stands teary-eyed,
full of the torture and anguish of prison grief, off to one side.
In a second there's an interruption, the sound of a prayerful
        bell,
and the bishop asks Odl, "What is your desire, pray tell?
What is your wish Jewish daughter Odl, I appeal to you,
speak in the last minute of your last day's ordeal
if you have a wish or desire. We shall fulfill anything—
except to save you from the fire!"

אָדל בת משה האָט זיך דאָס פּנים פֿאַרשטעלט:
באַדוויערט זי איצטער איר גיין פֿון דער וועלט?
אָדער איר מאַן וואָס בלײַבט מיט אַ קינד,
מיט איר טײַער, אי אײנציק, איר שוועלבעלע קינד
וואָס האָט נישט געפֿילט נאָך קיין טעם פֿון קיין זינד?
איר טאָטן דעם קצין? איר אָרעמע מאַמע,
דערלעבט איר אײנציקע טאָכטער צו זען אין פֿלאַמען?
איר לעבן וואָס ווערט איצט פֿאַרשניטן ווי אַ בוים
פֿינף און צוואַנציק יאָר אַלט זײַענדיק קוים,
נישט דאָס אַלץ באַטריבט און פֿאַרוואָלקנט דאָס געמיט
פֿון דער הײיליקער אָדל אין דער לעצטער מינוט
אַן אַנגסט האָט ווי אַ בליץ געשניטן אין געדאַנק:
— אַ טײַערע מענטשן הערט מײַן פֿאַרלאַנג —
האָט זיך אָדל בת משה צו די ריכטער געוווענדט:
איידער מײַן קערפּער וועט ווערן פֿאַרברענט
נאָך אַ פֿערד זיך נאָכשלעפֿן גאָס אײַן גאָס אויס,
קען דאָך אַ פֿאַרדעקט אָרט נאָך ווערן אַנטבלויזט
טאָ דערפֿילט מיר אַ טײַערע וואָס איך באַדאַרף
און נאָדלען דערלאַנגט מיר שפּיציקע שאַרף.

און ס׳האָט אָדל בת משה דעם זוים פֿון איר קלייד
מיט נאָדלען פֿאַרשטאָקן ווי ווײַט נאָר עס גייט
ביז די קנעכל פֿון די פֿיס צו פֿאַרדעקן דאָס לײַב
—נו איצט קענט איר דאָס פֿערדעלע טרײַבן
האָט דאָס געזיכט פֿון די קדושה געלויכטן פֿון פֿרייד
ביז ס׳האָט זיך די נשמה פֿון גוף אָפּגעשיידט...

Odl the daughter of Moyshe covered her face.
Does she now regret her departure from this place
or from her husband who remains with their child,
with her dear, her only, her mild swallow child,
who has not yet felt the taste of sin?
Or her father the Cohen, and her poor mother so thin,
who lived long enough to see her only daughter in flame,
her life now cut down like a tree, the pain
of her being burned at 25 years of age?
But that's not all that saddens and clouds the moral outrage
of the holy Odl, for in this last minute of time,
like lightning, angst cuts into thoughts of her crime:
"Oh dear people, listen to my wish."
Odl the daughter of Moyshe turned to the judges and said this:
"When my body is being dragged from street to street before it's
        burned,
I am so very concerned that a part of it might be exposed!
So, oh dear ones, heed me in what God knows is my last need:
Give me sharp needles, I plead!"

And Odl the daughter of Moyshe stitched the border of her dress to her ankles,
in order to cover her skin as much as possible,
and then said, "So, you can drive the little horse...."
And the face of the holy woman shone with joy,
Until in due course, the soul separated from her body.

שטיל־לאַנדשאַפֿט.

ווי הייליק שטיל איז איצט אויף פֿעלדער
ווי הייליק שטיל איז איצט די וועלט:—
און ווי אין פֿאָטער יעקבֿס חלום
וואָלט אַ לייטער זיין געשטעלט.

פֿון הימל ביז דער ערד אַ לייטער
מלאָכים גייען הין און צוריק
עס בלאָנדזשען מיינע פֿיס אויף ערד דאָ
און אין האַרצן—הימליש גליק...

46

Still Landscape

How sacred is the silence of fields now,
how sacred the silence of the world!—
And how, as in Father Jacob's dream,
a stairway heaps up

from earth toward heaven,
on which the angels go to and fro.
Though my legs have lost their way on earth,
In my heart—there is heavenly mirth...

זומער .

אַ יונגער שמעטערלינג נעכטן ערשט געבוירן
טראָגט אויף פֿליגלען גרינג זומערס גרויסע פֿרייד
דאָ דערפֿון אַ זאַם דאָרט אַ זאַם פֿארזייט
פֿליט ער זאַמלען פֿריש וואָס ער האָט פֿארלוירן...

פֿליט ער אויף און אָפ און ווייס נישט וואָס צו קלויבן:
אונטן גרינט דער מי זינגט אַ ים פֿון טענער
אויבן העלקייט קוועלט ווייס ער נישט וואָס שענער
צי פֿרייד די גרינע אונטן צי דאָס העלקייט אויבן...

איז אויף און אָפ, אַראָפ אַרויף און אומעטום אַ נאָג
פֿון דעם העלן ים און פֿון דעם גרינעם טאָל
אויף וועגן פֿרייד פֿארזייט און געקליבן אויף דאָס נײ.

אָ יונגער שמעטערלינג! דײַן לעבן איז אַ טאָג
און ס׳איז דײַן מילכל קליין און ס׳איז דײַן מאָגן שמאָל
פֿאַר אויסנאָגן ביז דנאָ די גאַנצע פֿרייד פֿון מיר!

48

Summer

Yesterday's newborn butterfly
carries summer's joy on its wings—
here a seed gathered, there a seed sowed,
always trying to garner another lost thing...

Rather unsure of what to gather, fluttering
as May greens below, singing a sea of notes,
while brightness beams beyond—the butterfly can't glean
what's lovelier, the joy below or the glow above...

Back and forth, up and down, it flits everywhere,
nibbling the bright sea, the greening valley—
joy resowed and gathered anew on the roadside ride.

Oh young butterfly—your life is a day,
your little mouth way too small, your tiny stomach too narrow
to gnaw out all the happiness of May!

אין דײַן קינדער-צימער

דאָס ליאַלקעלע האַלט אין דאָס געווײן אירס
ווײַל ס׳איז נעבעך טויט,
און שטעלט אויפֿן פּנימל אַ שמייכל פֿאַר דיר אָן.

דײַן פֿערדעלע מיטן אויסגעשטאָפּטן בויך פֿון שטרוי,
האָט נעבן דיר זיך אײַנגערעדט אַז עס לעבט,
נעם צו די פֿיסעלעך מײַן קינד עס זאָל דיר נישט פֿאַרטרעטן.

די לבֿנה אַנטלויפֿט פֿון דער וועלט אין דײַן צימערל אַרײַן,
זי האָט אַ פּנים פֿון אַ מענטש און שווערט זיך אַז זי איז אַ מענטש,
און מענטשן זאָגן אַז די אויגן אירע זענען בערגער
אָדער טיפֿע טאָלן
פֿון אַ פּלאַנעט אַן אָפּגעלאָשענעם...
אָבער דו מײַן קינד, דו גלייבסט איר אויפֿן וואָרט,
האָט זי דיך ליב און טרײַבט אַרויס
די נאַכט וואָס האָט זיך אײַנגעריכט מיט שוואַרץ
און שרעקט דיר אַ בער: אַ בער, אַ בער, אַ בער!...

50

In the Children's Room

The little doll holds back its crying
because she alas is dead
but has assumed on her small face
a smile for you.

Beside you the little horse, its belly stuffed with straw,
has convinced itself that it's alive—
move your little legs my child, so it will not trample you!

The moon runs away from the heavens
to your little room;
it also has a face
and swears that it's human,
although people say the eyes are mountains or deep valleys
of an extinguished planet;
but you my child take his word for it
so that he loves you and chases out
the night that blackened his soul with soot
and frightens you: A bear! A bear! A bear!

טריאָלעט.

האָסט אַליין דעם פלויט אויפֿן גרענעץ פֿון דײַן מאָרגן אויפֿגעשטעלט,
און אַליין די שטעכלדראָט אויף אים געדיכט פֿאַרצויגן,
עס זאָל דער ווינד אין ליב טיפֿער זײַן בײַם אַריבערבויגן,
איבערן פלויט וואָס דו האָסט אויפֿן גרענעץ פֿון דײַן מאָרגן אויפֿגעשטעלט.

דער זעלס קאָפריז: איר בענקשאַפֿט צו דער וועלט
זאָל ווי אַ קאָרן פֿון דער ערד אַרויסגעזויגן,
באַגראָבן זײַן אונטערן פלויט בײַם מאָרגן אויפֿגעשטעלט,
וואָס זי האָט אַליין אים מיט שטעכלדראָט פֿאַרצויגן...

52

Triolet

You yourself erected the fence on the border of your tomorrow
and alone pulled tightly, densely the barbed wire
to more deeply wound your flesh when you bend
over the fence you yourself erected on the border of your
        tomorrow.

Ah the soul's caprice: her yearning for the world!
May the corn be sucked out of the earth
from under the fence erected at tomorrow
by she herself who pulled tight the barbed wire.

אַ גרוס.

דעם ליבשאַפֿטסגרוס וואָס עס אַנט דאָס בלוט אין מיר,
האָט מיר אַ שטראַל געברענגט פֿון אַ וויַיטן שטערן,
צוריק צוויי טויזנט יאָר האָט דאָרט אַ קרעכץ געלאָזן הערן,
און ס׳טראָגט דער שטראַל אים ערשט אויף דער שוועל פֿאַר מיַין טיר.

מיַין ליבשאַפֿטסגרוס אַ טראָג מיַין שטראַל צוריק!
ביז דו וועסט וועמען אין דיַין לויף דערגרייכן.
וויַיס איך וויַיל אַז ס׳וועט שוין דאַן קיין ציַיכן,
נישט זיַין, נישט פֿון מיַין צער און נישט פֿון מיַין גליק.

דאָך די זאל נאָכן טיפֿסטן גליק אומרויִק,
מיינט, אַז וויַיל זי איז פֿרעמד און נישט דאַיִק,
מוז זי אַוודאַי אַ שטאַמלונג זיַין פֿון אַ וויַיטן שטערן.

און דער ציטער אירער און דאָס אייביק גאָרן,
וויַיל זי געדענקט איר אַלטע ליבשאַפֿט נאָך און קען זיך גענאַרן,
זי האָט ווען געלעבט אין די וויַיטע ספֿערן!

Hour of All Hours

The love message my blood still senses within me
has travelled from a far away star.
A thousand years ago, someone there sighed deeply,
and now that pain is first being beamed to my doorstep.

Oh star of mine, carry my message of love
back along the reaches of your path.
I only know, at that moment,
no sign will remain of either my sorrow or my happiness.

Yet even in that hour of all hours, a portent of our souls will still exist—
as if in the moment the soul's unbound from the body,
it might assume the shape of an innocent from on high.

Oh this age-old trembling—this everlasting desire,
but still smitten with old love, she who once dwelt in the upper spheres,
shall not allow herself to be captured by the star's shimmering, illusionary light.

ס׳טרעפֿט אַז אויך אין אָבֿ פֿאַלט אַ מאָל צו אַזוי די נאַכט
ווי אַ לײַלעך אויף אַ גוסס־פּנים,
ס׳האָט פֿרי ווער האַרבסט געמאַכט, פֿון זײַערע קבֿרים
שרײַען בלומען אַרויס: מיר לעבן דאָך נאָך!

און די וועלט איז פֿול געוויין ווי אויף אַ שווערן בראָך,
ווי קוילן פֿאַלן פֿייגל פֿון אַלע צווײַגן אַראָפּ,
אין אַזאַ נאַכט צילט די וועלט זיך אין איר אייגענעם קאָפּ,
שוואַרצע טײכן רינען פֿון אירע שלייפֿן.

Untitled

Also it sometimes happens that night falls
like a sheet over a person who has just died.
Somebody has made autumn come early,
though from their graves flowers are yelling—
       "We are still alive!"

But the world is crying as if for a disaster,
and birds tumble from branches like bullets.
On a night such as this, the earth aims at her own
head and black rivers flow from her temples.

מײַן טאַטע.

I

ס׳איז אַזאַ מאָדנער טרויער דאָ אינעם נאָך־פּסחדיקן ווינט,
וואָס ברומט ווי אַ יעשענגנאַכט אין לאָדן שטיל אַרײַן,
ס׳איז מוצאי־יום־טובֿ, די באָבע גייט אַנטקעגן
דעם זומער מיט אַ זיפֿץ און אַ שטיל געבעט,
אין ווירוואַר פֿון בין־הזמנים מישט מײַן לעבן זיך
ווי אַ בוך וואָס לופֿטערט זיך אין ווינט,
דעמאָלט גראָבט מײַן האַרץ די שוואַרצקייט פֿון דער נאַכט
ווי אַ קרעט, די ערד אויס בילדערהייט.
ווערט מאָדנע נאָענט נאָענט צו דיר דער וועג, צו דיר, עלנטער טאַטע מײַנער
צו דײַן קבֿר וואָס שטייט שוין פֿערצן יאָר,
אַזוי אַ בערגל זאַמד אָן אַ אויסקריץ אויף אַ שטיין,
און מײַן קאָפּ בייגט זיך איבערן קבֿר אַריבער
און שרײַט אין אים אַרײַן:
— טאַטע! טאַטע!

58

My Father

I

Such an odd sadness this wind
on the eighth night of Passover—
electrically charged as if it were already autumn
so that grandmother greets it with sighs and laments.

A wind that races thru the seasons of the year
as tho' it were flapping pages in the Book of Life—
until my heart claws at the blackness of night
like a mole burrowing blindly into the earth...

Oh lonely father of mine this road comes
strangely close to wherever your grave may be—
a small quicksand mound with a vanishing inscription
lost these fourteen years...

My head would collapse over your grave
and shout into it—Father, Father!

די נאַכט ווי אַ פֿאַרבלאָטיקטע מגילה,

פֿון דײַנע ליידן האָט זיך אויפֿגעוויקלט,

און ווערטער קוים לעזבאַרע פֿינקלען פֿון די שטערן:

רבינס הויף... אַ גאָון... וווּטער זענען בלויזן,

ס׳האָט עמעץ דאָ געלייענט, געגאַסן טײַכן טרערן,

אַן איינציק קינד געהאַט... אַוועק פֿרעסן הויזן

אין שאַפּ, געבענקט, געליטן,

טרויעריק געוווען זײַן לעבן, נאָך טרויעריקער זײַן שטאַרבן

(נישט אַלע מענטשן שנײַדן פֿון פֿרייד די גאָרבן),

מאַונט סיני האָספּיטאַל, בראַנד, צוויי יאָרן לייד,

און צו דער מגילה איז צוגעשפּיליעט דער טויטנשײַן.

Standard Sertyficate of death:

Nr. Nr. 16.345

לאָמור, צו זאָגן דיר אַז אַמעריקע איז נישט קיין קעלישקל רויטער ווײַן...

נאָר איך קוק אין טויטשײַן און זוך אַן ענטפֿער דאָרט:

איך בין אַ קינד געוווען בײַ דיר דײַן אַוועקפֿאָר און וווּניק דיך געקענט,

נאָר דײַן גרויסקייט ווערט דערצײַלט דאָ אונטער אַלע ווענט,

איינער זאָגט נאָך דײַנס אַ פּשט אין אַ שווער שטיקל ”עקידה”,

אַ צווייטער דײַן חריפֿותדיקן ”כאַפּ” און ”מודה” אויסווייניק,

אַ דריטער ווייס אַז אויך אין ניסתּר האָסטו געהאַט אַ האַנט,

אַ פֿערטער לויבט זיך גאָר פֿון דײַן האַרץ נישט אָפּ

וואָס האָט אַ לעצטן גראָשן זײַנעם געקענט צעטיילן,

נאָר אויף אַלעם ווייס די טויטשײַן אַזוי וווּניק צו דערצײַלן

און ווייס פֿון דײַן לעבן דאָס אָפֿיציעלע נאָר:

Trade, profession or particular kind of work:

PRESSER...

II

This night like the bloodied Megillah of Esther
barely discernible words radiate until they reveal your
suffering like stars from afar in the rabbi's courtyard where
some still claim your genius, and their torrential tears
saturate the sacred pages with bubbles...

Someone speaks of your interpretations of a difficult section,
the attempted sacrifice of Isaac and Abraham.
A second extols your profound grasp and explanations by heart.
The third believes you even had a hand in the mystical Kabbalah.
A fourth can't stop praising your kindness, how you'd share your last zloty...

But surely your stature arises not from these heights
but from underneath the low walls of your despair
for not all people are cut from sheaves of joy
some go against the grain... I was a child when you left
who barely knew you when you fled to press pants in a shop...

Perhaps you yearned for your family, had a sad life, and a sadder death.
But I only know what is official about your life: Mt Sinai Hospital.
The official stamp on a standard Death Certificate—*#16.345. Trade: Presser*

And so to the Megillah is affixed
a deadly glow as if to say that all of America can't
substitute for a small glass of ceremonial wine.

Notes to Section I

"The Ballad of Odl": A retelling of the Peretz folktale.

"Still Landcape": The dying Isaac blesses his son and says "Ah! the smell of my son is like the smell of open country blessed by the Lord. God gives you dew from heaven and the richness of the earth..." (Genesis, Chapter 27.)

"Jacob's dream" – In ancient belief, deities revealed themselves by dream at sacred sites. The imagery in Jacob's dream is derived from the Babylonian ziggurat or temple tower, 'with the top in the sky', and with brick steps leading up to a small temple at the top. (Genesis, Chap. 28: 12, The New English Bible, Oxford Univ. Press, 1976.)

"a stairway heaps up" – Stairway is the correct word in Hebrew: Sullam. Traditionally but inaccurately translated as ladder. From the verb salal, to heap up, such as dust. (Genesis, Chapter 28: 12, footnote 27, 1-45, The New American Bible, Nelson, 1983.)

"I the Lord...am the God of your forefather Abraham and the God of Isaac,... the land on which you are lying I will give to you and your descendants. These shall be as plentiful as the dust of the earth..." Genesis, Chapter 28.

Jacob and his mother, the instigator of the plot to deceive Esau and Isaac, are condemned by Jeremiah, Hosea, and Yahwist, etc. They pay for it by life-long separation from each other. The story also is told as part of the mystery of God's ways in salvation—his use of weak sinful men to achieve his own ultimate purpose." (The New American Bible, Genesis, Chapter 27, 28, 29, footnote 27:1-45).

"In the Children's Room": In Yiddish "moon" is feminine, "horse" neuter, "doll" neuter and/or feminine.

"My Father": Megillah: Biblical story of Esther. Emiot had several different handwritten stanza variations of this poem.

Section II

1940–1957

Kazhkstan, Moscow, Birobidjhan, Siberia, USSR

From Lider, Rising, *and* Yearning

EMIOT FLED THE GERMAN INVASION of Poland in 1939, and worked briefly at a radio station in nearby Bialystok, Russia, until transported, like many refugees, including his wife and children, east to a work camp in Kazakhstan. His mother remained in Poland, where she became a Holocaust victim. Emiot's train was bombed. Living conditions in Kazakhstan were dire. "A Prayer in Nineteen Forty-Three" documents these conditions, and was possibly the only identifiable poem he wrote there. Emiot chose to open his book called Siberia with this poem, although the book is actually about his Gulag years. Soon thereafter he was somehow able to travel to Moscow, where he lived from 1940 to 1944.

The details of that transition are vague at best. Suffice to say that during those years Stalin was engaged in cordial cultural relationships with Jews, partly in order to encourage the Allies to join the wartime effort against Hitler's Germany. The Moscow-originated Joint Anti-Fascist Committee, by then a worldwide endeavor, sent Emiot to Birobidjhan as a journalist in 1944. Birobidjhan was the first Autonomous Jewish Republic, established during this period by Stalin. However, in 1948, Emiot was sent from Birobidjhan to a Gulag in Siberia for crimes of "internationalism." This occurred during the reversal of pro-Jewish thinking by Stalin and others, during which time Jewish doctors, artists, writers, filmmakers, scientists, etc., were imprisoned and/or murdered during a now infamous reign of terror.

Emiot's book, *Lider* (Song/Poem), published in Moscow in 1940 by the government publisher, had an Introduction by an approved literary critic. It is both excessively laudatory and condescending, exclaiming that Emiot had been saved by Soviet society from his prior Jewish, and Polish-Jewish religious, bourgeois, self-absorbed thinking and writing. The Introduction was obviously required as a condition of publication. Yet it directly contradicts the content of the book itself. Moreover, Emiot, like any talented writer, managed to write richly and ambiguously enough to allow for dual meanings for diverse readers. Nevertheless, the Introduction insists that, "Emiot said goodbye to one world and greeted another....Emiot is a lyricist...who had bumped up against the mercilessness and tiresome, boring, disgusting ruling robbers of society...the autumn wind for him was full of 'father-pity' and 'mother-melody'…the poet fears he will not live long enough to express the richness of Soviet concepts."

Leaving aside a few patriotic poems pertinent to the war effort, *Lider* is a book which presents some of Emiot's most brilliant, worldly, sophisticated, and diverse poems: "Chinese Man" is a long narrative poem which deals with the political vacillations and allegiances between China, Japan and Russia in the late 1930s by personalizing the events and thus conveying a vivid portrait of a human being by both description and dialogue. Five poems deal with music, and not just as a passing or even an extended metaphor: "On Seeing La Gioconda" is a sensuous poem that brings to life an historic personage with exacting detail. In "On Hearing Chopin," Emiot argues that "happiness is our destiny," and thus "adorned with music." Then, harkening back to his childhood, Emiot asks in "Just So," who needs Chopin, Hayden or Mozart if we have the melody of the cradle of the gate, the language of the tin roof? Another sensuous poem titled "Tamara Hanum," who was a famous Uzbeki-stani dancer, insists that watching her has forever transformed and freed him. Finally, "My Premonition of a Lullaby" is a lament addressed to a lost and/or absent love, using the cunning pseudo-logic of nature and despair. All these are people poems, and one also suspects that despite wartime circumstances, Emiot was able to partake of some major cultural opportunities and new friendships in the capitol city during these years.

Another poem titled "Before Spring" appears in *Lider* for the first time, but is republished by Emiot in at least three other venues in later years. In it, despite every difficult aspect of his life and times, "the hum of spring and tug of breezes will lead him forward into…spring's suffusing smile."

By contrast, the yoke of his official assignment sits heavily upon his literary shoulders in the book called Rising, published in Birobidjhan in 1947. Three factors account for this: Stalin's growing paranoia about Jews, the energy and enthusiasm that actually did exist amongst Jewish settlers in Biro-bidjhan, and Emiot's perhaps subsequent artistic constraints as he at the same time functioned as a journalist in a strange, and largely rural environment. A poem titled "In the Hospital" recounts the tale of a blinded but doggedly patriotic soldier who is overjoyed that "… the enemy has retreated from Mos-cow." Another poem, "Sholem Aleykem Street," celebrates the main street in Birobidjhan being named after the legendary Yiddish writer, which the poem insists could only happen in a Soviet location… The poem "A Fall Like This Anywhere Else?" uses a musical metaphor to celebrate life in Birobidjhan, and allows Emiot to return to his more natural lyricism. But alas, by 1948 Emiot would have been spared trial in Moscow as a spy for the USA, been incarcerated in a Siberian Gulag, and been lucky not to have been murdered.

During the seven years of his ten-year sentence to hard labor in a Gulag, Emiot secretly wrote poems which he largely hid on cigarette papers or memorized. However, these poems were not published (and later republished) until after he left Poland for the United States. (1961 *In Melody Absorbed*, later in *Before You Extinguish Me*, 1966.)

After the Gulag he returned to Birobidjhan. Archives there describe him as nearly naked and barefoot, a shadow of himself in ill health. Eventually because of his Polish citizenship, he was eligible for rehabilitation in the famous Medem Sanitorium in Warsaw. Emiot published a book in Warsaw in 1957 called *Yearning*. Understandably, the tone of the collection is overall somber and bereft. However, some of the manuscript has been lost. A slightly altered version of the poem called "Just Like This" can be found in the stray poems in Section IV of this book. A poem titled "Melody" describes a relationship in an extended musical metaphor. The poem entitled "Stores" uses a well-known folksong called "The Store-Keeper" as the foundation for a poem about the choices we make and are made for us by life. (This poem is also reproduced with almost no modification in *Before You Extinguish Me*.) An untitled poem, essentially another address to God, is also based on a classic Chassidic dudele or song-to-God form. It is one of his more mystical prayers, as befits the essentially religious dudele. A strong wartime theme characterizes the poem "Umschlagplatz in Warsaw," the famous Nazi transport gathering site for trains to death camps. It is one of Emiot's few existing poems that directly express his anger and horror at the war itself. "Tango" extends that tone by saying that ("whether it's death/or life that gives you a kiss, things will be okay.") In Yiddish the cadence of the Tango is evident. But the poem "Strangers" reminds us how illusive and fragile happiness had become for Emiot. Although Emiot had many difficult memories of Siberia, his poem "In The Village" extols simple peasant village life and wishes he could whole-heartedly participate in its youthful pleasures. Originally this last poem was part of the Siberian cycle, but probably was judged by Emiot as essentially too optimistic to remain in that cycle. The book *Yearning*, with its many fluctuations in mood, despite its incomplete manuscript, should be viewed as coming from a time of enormous transition in Emiot's life.

א כינעזער

ער האָט אָפּגעשוירן זײַן צאָפּ, ער טראָגט נישט די
סאַנדאַלן.
אַ האַרטער הוט, אַ רעגן־מאַנטל און פּיין־לאַקירטע שיך,
מיט צוויי טשעמאָדאַנען איבער וואָקזאַלן
דעם נאָענטסטן וועג צום שטעטל פֿרעגט ער מיך.

פֿון זײַן לאַנד געבליבן אים זײַן טונקל־ברוינע הויט,
די קליינע אויגן פֿאַרחלומטע, זײַן נידעריק געשטאַלט.
וויל איך אָפּנעמען פֿון זײַן לאַנד דעם גרוס פֿון דער
נויט
און אַלץ, וואָס די אומעטיקע אויגן זײַנע שטיל אין
זיך פֿאַרבאַהאַלטן.

נאָר דאָ איז ער סוחר איצט. זײַן נאָמען: סען־יון־
טאַנג.
אפֿשר דאַרף איך קרעלן שײַנע פֿון זײַן וווּנדערלאַנד,
באַסלעטן, קעמלעך פֿאַר זיך צי פֿאַר געשאַנק,
בורשטינען, זילבעררינגען, פּערל אַלעראהאַנט?
ער זאָגט, און ער עפֿנט אויף די פֿאַרשטויבטע
טשעמאָדאַנען, —
איך קען קויפֿן אָדער אויף אַ ציונגס־קוויטל דאָס אַלץ געוווינען,
נאָר פּלוצעם, איך וויס אַליין נישט פֿון וואָס און
פֿון וואַנען:
—זאָגט, אַ, ליבער מענטש, וואָס הערט מען איצט אין כינע?

ער פֿרעגט, און די אויגן זײַנע קאָנוווּלסיוו צעציטערט
הייבן בלאָנדזשען אָן איבערן ווילדן וואַלד פֿון די
ווערטער אין מײַן ציַיטונג
—איז אמת, אַז פּעקין איז שוין איצט דערשיטערט
פֿון שׁונאַס קויל, און דער חורבן גייט וויַיטער אַלץ
און וויַיטער?

Chinese Man

He's cut his braid and discarded his sandals
for a stiff hat, raincoat, and patent leather shoes.
Carrying two suitcases through the train station,
he asks me about the nearest road to town.

All that is left to him from his homeland is
dark brown skin, small dreamy eyes, and short stature,
while the news of the emergency in his land has taken hold of me
with everything that his sad, silent eyes hide inside.

He's a traveling salesman now, named Sen-Yun-Tang:
Perhaps I need beautiful beads from his exotic land,
bracelets, combs—for myself or as a gift—
amber, silver rings, or various kinds of pearls?

He opens his dusty valises, saying
I can buy now or win all later in a lottery;
when suddenly, out of nowhere, he asks,
"Oh tell me my dear man, what's the news from China?"

His eyes flutter convulsively, wandering
the wilderness of my newspaper's words:
—"is it true Peking has now been shocked
by thousands of enemy bullets, and the havoc goes on and on?"

און אויב איך בין אַ גוטער מענטש, און בין עס דאָך מסתמא,

טאָ וויזן אים דעם קירצסטן וועג אין זײַן לאַנד צו קומען.

צען לײַבן רײַסן זיך אין האַרץ זײַנס אויף נקמה,

רײַסן זיך ווי פֿון אַ שטײַג און ברומען.

שטײ איך אַזוי מיט סען־יון־טאַנג מיט זײַנע טשעמאָדאַנען

און זוך דעם וועג צום וווּטן לאַנד און קען אים נישט געפֿינען,

נאָר איבער מײַנע פֿאַרחלומטע צניעותדיקע לאַנען,

גיסט די זון אין עמערס אויס דאָס רויטע בלוט פֿון כינע.

And if I am a good person, and of course, perhaps I am,
I should show him the shortest route home,
since in his heart ten lions strive for revenge,
strive to rip open their cage and roar!

So I stand with Sen-Yun-Tang and his suitcases
and seek out the path to that distant land in vain,
while over the dreamlike innocence of nature
the sun pours, as if from a pail, the red blood of China.

1938

זי לעבט נאָך, מײַסטער, יונג אין אַלע פֿאַרבן,
זי טראָגט נאָך דין איר שמייכל און איר לוסט,
נאָך ווייעט לײַכט דער שטאָלצער גלוסט
איבער צײַט און איבער שטאַרבן.

נאָך ווײַנט דער ניגון שטיל אַרום די קאַרבן
פֿון געוואַנט, וואָס האַלדזט אַרום די ברוסט,
ס׳איז נאָך שטיין געבליבן לײַכט פֿאַרדרוס
אַרום געזיכט פֿון געדאַנקען בײַזע, האַרבע.

אָט באַלד—און דער שפּרוך פֿון די קאָלירן
וועט אַן עפֿן טאָן געהיימע וויטע טירן,
די שיינקייט וועט שענער ווערן, שענער!

אַ, מײַסטער, וואָס איז פֿאַרגאַנג און שטאַרבן,
ווען טעענער פֿאַרגייען זיך אין פֿאַרבן
און פֿאַרבן פֿאַרגייען שטיל אין טעענער?

[דזשאָקאָנדאַ—דאָס באַקאַנטע בילד פֿון לעאָנאַרדאָ דאַ ווינטשי]

On Seeing La Gioconda

Master, she still lives, her flesh still vibrant,
still carrying that slight smile,
that proud desire that gently transcends
both time and her death.

Still the melody softly wafts from
the layers of fabric that bind
her breasts unto their cleavage,
though a gentle remnant of resentment,
a puzzling thought, suffuses her face.

But soon the incantation of colors
will open secret, distant doors
and her beauty will become still more lovely.

Oh Master, what is gone is indeed dead,
but it has been transformed by your brushstrokes
into traces of living flesh.

1940

הערנדיק שאָפּענען

1

זאָל דאָס זײַן דאָס גליק, וואָס איז אונדז ווען באַשערט:
פֿילן אין זיך, ווי לעבן און טויט זיך טוישן,
ווי גוט איז אויפֿן שטילסטן טאָג צו לוישן,
ווי אַן עכאָ, דעם אָפּקלאַנג פֿון דער ערד.

עס האַלט דעם אָטעם אײַן די נאַכט און הערט,
און אַלע קוואַלן מוזן שטילער רוישן,
טויזנט ליבשאַפֿטן און טויזנט מאָל אַנטוישן,
טויזנט מאָל געבויעט און טויזנט מאָל צעשטערט.

זאָל דאָס זײַן דאָס גליק, מיט צוגעלענטע וויִעס זען די
וועלט,
אַלע נעפּלען שײַנען איצט צעהעלט,
האַרץ צו האַרץ שלאָגן איצט דערנעבן,
וועלט מיט וועלט, ווי בלעטער אין אַ בוך פֿאַרוועגדט,
שטייך האָט אינעם מענטש זײַן פֿאַטער ערשט דערקענט,
און פֿול איז אַלץ מיט פֿאַרגעבן און פֿאַרגעבן.

וויִג אײַן די וועלט ווי שטיל צעוויגטן גראַז,
אָוונט וועט דעם לעצטן רויש פֿאַרמעקן,
זע: דער בלינדער וואַרפֿט אַוועק דעם שטעקן
און קוקט דורך דער מויערוואַנט ווי דורך אַ גלאָז.

דער חכם פֿרעגט מער נישט, פֿאַר וואָס
דער האָן האָט אויפֿגעהערט צו וועקן,
דאָס פֿיקסל האָט אויפֿגעהערט צו שרעקן
אין וואַלד דעם ציטערדיקן האָז.

On Hearing Chopin

Is this the happiness that is our destiny—
this feeling that life and death trade places?
How good it is to listen on the stillest of days
when like an echo, the earth reverberates.

Night holds its breath and listens,
and all the wells gurgle more quietly,
as a thousand loves, a thousand sorrows
are a thousand times created, a thousand times destroyed.

May this close-lashed happiness make possible
a new vision of the world
in which all fogs lift
and heart unto heart beat in unison,
and like leaves, worlds within worlds are transformed into a book,
stone has just now recognized his father in man,
and all is full with forgiving and forgiveness.

Put the world to sleep like quietly swaying grass;
evening will erase the last sounds.
Look: the blind man discards his cane
and sees through a brick wall as though it were glass.

No more does the wise man ask why;
the rooster has ceased to wake,
the fox to frighten
and the forest's rabbit to tremble.

קום, לעבן, דו אויסגעבענקטס און שיינס,
ס'איז די וועלט געצירט פֿאַר דיר מיט טענער,
ווי אויף פֿאַראַד קלינגט אַ וויטער גלאָק—די צײַט.

מיר ווילן הערן, הערן, וואָס איבער אַלע שטערן.
ס'איז דאָס לעבן קליין—מיר האָבן גרעסערע באַגערן,
און יעדער אונדזער אָטעם—אייביקייט.

Come life, you are longed for and beautiful!
For you the world is adorned with music
which sounds time's distant parade-like bell.

We so want to hear—to hear that which is beyond all stars—
for life is so brief, our desires so immense,
and our every breath an eternity.

1935

דאַרפֿסטו שאַפֿען, צי היידן, צי מאַצאַרטן דערצו?
גענוג אַ מאָל דער ניגון אין שטילן וויג פֿון טויער,
ס׳זאָל דיר קלאָר ווערן מיט אַ מאָל דער גאַנצער וויי און
טרויער

פֿון באַשאַף. דאַרפֿסטו שאַפֿען דען, צי היידן, צי
מאַצאַרטן דערצו?
ער דערצײײלט דעם וועלט־צער דיר אויך אין אַ פֿראָסטן
אינדערפֿרי

די שפּראַך פֿון בלעך אויפֿן דאַך,
וואָס הייבט זיך און פֿאַלט אַראָפּ ערגעץ אויף דײַן מויער,
פֿון ווינט באַוועגט. דאַרפֿסטו שאַפֿען דען, צי היידן, צי
מאַצאַרטן דערצו?
גענוג אַ מאָל דער ניגון אינעם שטילן וויג פֿון טויער.

Just So

Who needs Chopin, or Hayden, oh, even Mozart;
the melody of the quiet cradle of the gate is sometimes enough
to make clear the entire pain and sadness of creation;
do you need Chopin, Hayden, or Mozart too?

Also on an ordinary morning, proof of the world's sorrow is spoken
by the language of your tin roof
as it lifts and falls here and there upon your dwelling with the wind;
who then needs Chopin, Hayden or Mozart;
the melody in the quiet cradle of the gate is sometimes enough.

צו טאַמאַרא כאנום

טרעפֿט אַ מאָל אַ האָגענקריי אין בײַטאָגן,
קרייט ער אויס דעם עלנט פֿון דער וועלט.
אַ ווײַטער רויש פֿון אַ פֿאָרנדיקן וואָגן,
אַ ווינט, וואָס כאַפֿט דאָס אומעטיקע נאָגן
פֿון אַ ניגון אין דרויסן אויף דער קעלט.

טרעפֿט אַ מאָל, אַ האָנטדרוק שטיל אָן ווערטער
דײַן לעבן דערצײַילט דיר אויף אַ מאָל,
דײַן ליבשאַפֿט דערשטיקטע און באַגערטע,
דײַן צוקונפֿט אין ווײַטסטער ווײַט באַשערטע,
דײַן יוגנטס פֿרילינגדיקער קול.

כ׳האָב קיין ווערט פֿאַר פֿלאַמיקע געפֿילן,
פֿאַר דײַן געזאַנג פֿון פֿעלקערלעכן טאַנץ,
פֿון מײַן היים פֿון דבֿיקותדיקער תפֿילה,
פֿון תעניתים, פֿון כל־נידרי און פֿון נעילה
צו דײַן שטאַם געוווען ווײַט דער וועג און לאַנג.

נאָר בלויז די וואָר אַליין, די האָט דערנעענטערט,
וואָס חלום צעטיילט האָט מיט אַ ים,
נאָר בלויז די וואָר האָט צענומען אַלע ווענט דאָרט,
געענדערט דאָס, וואָס באַדאַרף ווערט זײַן געענדערט,
צו דיר אַליין און צו דײַן ווײַטן שטאַם.

80

Tamara Hanum

It happens sometimes that a rooster crows at dawn
about the loneliness of the world, or there is the
distant creak of a moving wagon, or a cold wind
catches the haunting gnaw of a melody.

It happens sometimes that a silent touch of the hand
reveals all at once how in my life of previously
stifled desires, your song has transformed
and released me like the suddenness of spring.

I find no words for these enflamed feelings;
in my own tradition I have only known songs of fasting,
of prayers for the dead, or the final prayer of atonement—
surely from you the path has been distant and long.

But suddenly your reality has come closer,
has torn down the walls within me, you
and you alone, with your exotic origins, has released
that which will have to be changed within me.

מײַן וויגליד-אַנען

און ווײַל עס וועלן אַלע בלומען
דאָך ווען פֿאַרוועלקטע שטיין,
אַזוי געל פֿאַרוועלקטע שטיין,
פֿיל איך שוין, ווי אַלע בלומען
געל פֿאַרוועלקטע שטיין,
געל פֿאַרוועלקטע שטיין.

און ווײַל עס וועלן פֿון די ביימער
בלעטער זיכער פֿאַלן,
עלנט בלעטער פֿאַלן,
פֿיל איך שוין, ווי פֿון ביימער
עלנט בלעטער פֿאַלן,
עלנט בלעטער פֿאַלן.

און ווײַל ערגעץ וועט אַ ווינט דאָך,
אַ שנייווינט זיכער בלאָזן,
אַזוי טונקל גרויזאַם בלאָזן,
הער איך שוין דעם שנייווינט
אַזוי טונקל גרויזאַם בלאָזן,
אַזוי טונקל זרויזאַם בלאָזן.

און ווײַל פֿון מיר צו דיר דער וועג איז
אַ טויזנט וויאַרסטן לאַנג,
אַ טויזנט וויאַרסטן לאַנג,
פֿיל איך נעבן דיר דעם וועג
טויזנט וויאַרסטן לאַנג,
טויזנט וויאַרסטן לאַנג.

My Premonition of a Lullaby

And because all the flowers will
certainly at some time become wilted
and remain a withered yellow,
I already feel as though
the flowers have already wilted,
and will remain a withered yellow.

And because the leaves from
the trees will certainly fall,
      these lonely leaves that will fall,
I already feel as though
      these leaves have fallen from the trees
      these lonely leaves have already fallen.

And because somewhere a wind,
a snowy wind will certainly blow,
      darkly, savagely, cruelly blow—
I already hear that snowy wind
      darkly, savagely, cruelly blowing,
      darkly, savagely, cruelly blowing.

And because from me to you
      the road is a thousand versts
      a thousand versts too long,
I feel near to you even though
      a thousand versts is very long,
      a thousand versts is so very long.

און וויל איך וועל דיך זיכער
קיין מאָל, קיין מאָל זען,
קיין מאָל מער ניט זען,
פֿיל איך טיף אַזוי,
ווי איך וועל דיך קיין מאָל זען,
קיין מאָל מער ניט זען.

און וויל מײַן געזיכט אין די דלאָניעס
וועט אַוודאי פֿאַרגראָבן זײַן,
מיט געוויין פֿאַרגראָבן זײַן,
פֿיל איך שוין ס׳געוויין מײַן
אין די דלאָניעס פֿאַרגראָבן זײַן,
אין די דלאָניעס פֿאַרגראָבן זײַן.

—הערסטו, נאַרעלע מײַנס,
—הערסטו, טײַערע מײַן?
—"טשודנאָי טשעלאָוועק!"...

And because I probably will
never see you again
never ever see you,
I feel even more deeply certain that
       I will never see you again,
       never see you ever again.

And since my face will be buried
in the palm of my hand
       I will certainly be buried,
will be buried sobbing and so
I already feel my weeping
       my face buried in the palm of my hands
       my face buried in the palm of my hands.

—Do you hear, my dear, foolish little one?
—Do you hear, my dearest, foolish little one?
—" You wonderful person, you…"

1940

פֿאַר פֿרילינג

וועליק צי אפֿשר ניט וועליק,
אזוי ווייט דעם האַרצן און פֿרעמד,
פֿארן ליכטיק צעשמייכלטן פֿרילינג
עס האָט מײַן געמיט זיך פֿאַרשעמט.

ס׳איז אזוי פֿיל פֿאַרבײ און עס קומט נאָך,
נאָר אין מיר, ווי שטיל איז, ווי שטיל!
אמאָליק אזוי עס ברומט נאָך
ווי אַ טויב דער יונגער אַפֿריל.

ווער ווייסט פֿון וואָן די בעריאָזע
וויגט אַ גרוס מיר מיט צווייגן פֿאַרדאַרט?
אין די שויבן פֿון פֿרילינג די ראָזע
ווי אין די ראָזיקע שויבן פֿון האַרבסט.

ס׳איז ערגעץ פֿאַרפֿרוירן מײַן חלום
אין ווינטער אויף שניי און אויף אײַז,
ערשט שלעפֿן ווינטלעך בײַ פֿאַלעס
ווי קינדער אַן אַנטינקן גרײַז...

זיי וועלן אים ערגעץ דערפֿירן
אויף וועגן, ווער ווייסט ווהין—
אויף פֿעלדער אים ערגעץ פֿאַרלירן
בײַ פֿײגל, בײַ ביימער, בײַ גרינס...

86

Before Spring

Willingly, perhaps unwillingly,
despite my alienated and remote heart,
spring's suffusing smile
shames my spirits.

So much has passed and is still to come,
but within me how quiet it is, so quiet
at times young April hums
like a dove!

Somewhere, my dream is frozen
in a winter of snow and ice,
but how these breezes tug at the flaps of my overcoat,
like children urging on a frosty-haired elder.

They will lead him somewhere,
on who knows what paths,
and there lose him in the fields
among trees, among birds, among meadows.

אין שפּיטאָל

מײַן שכן, דער יונגער לייטענאַנט,
האָט זיך אַ זעץ געטאָן אויפֿן באַנק בײַם ראַנד,
האָט אַ ריס געטאָן פֿון אויגן די באַנדאַזשן.
די שוועסטער האָט אים צוגעשמידט צום וואַנט,
באַפֿוילן אים: ליגן נאָך אַנאַנד,
אַפֿילו דעם פּנים זיך נישט וואַשן.

די שוועסטער — פֿון שרעק בלייך און ווײַס:
— יונגער מענטש, ווי באַגייט מען אַזאַ גרײַז?
אַ טראָפּן שײַן איז סם דאָך פֿאַר די אויגן,
נאָר ער גיט בלינדערהייט אַ ווײַז
אין צײַטונג אויף דער פֿאַרגעלייענטער נײַס —
דער שונא איז פֿון מאָסקווע אָפּגעצויגן.

און פֿון האַרץ גיט אַ ריס זיך אַ געזאַנג —
ער מוז אַוודאי זיצן אין געדאַנק
אין זײַן טאַנק אויף שטורעם אָנגעצויגן.
זע: אָט פֿלאַמט שוין אויף זײַן טאַנק,
נאָר ער — ער רוט נישט אַזוי לאַנג,
ביז דער פֿלאַם פֿאַרנעמט נישט זײַנע אויגן.

88

In the Hospital

My neighbor, the young lieutenant,
grabs a seat on the edge of the bench
and pulls the bandage from his eyes;
the nurse nails him to the wall,
orders him to lie there
not even to wash his face!

Pale-white from fear, she says,
"Young man how can you make such a mistake;
you know even a drop of light is poison for your eyes."
But he only gestures blindly toward the paper
from which the news was read aloud
that the enemy has retreated from Moscow.

And a song rips itself from his heart,
for in memory he is sitting there
in his tank amid the battle's storm...
Look: Already the tank's ablaze,
and he—he must not stay there
until the flames seize his eyes!

שלום־עליכם־גאַס

נישט ווי ס׳איז ביי אים אין די ביכער קלוג באַשריבן,
נישט דיך האָט ער מיט זיין געלעכטער אויסגעלאַכט,
זיין גרויסער נאָמען איז פֿאַרקניפּט מיט דיר פֿאַרבליבן,
ווייל אַזוי האָט ער געהאָפֿט, אַזוי האָט ער געדאַכט.

אַזוי האָט אַ גאַס אַ ייִדישע איר תּיקון
אָפּגעפֿונען אין בויונג און אין טאַט,
אַ גאַס, וואָס זאָל פֿול זיין מיט פֿאַבריקן:
״רעטאַל״, ״דימיטראָוו״, וועבער־קאָמבינאַט.

מיט מחנות, וואָס ציִען צו דער אַרבעט אין פֿאַרטאָגן,
און עס באַגלייט געזאַנג זיי אין דער וויַיט,
נאָר אַזאַ גאַס איז דיין נאָמען ווערט צו טראָגן
אַ, מייסטער, אין דער טיפֿער אייביקייט!

90

Sholem Aleykhem Street

His great name remains bound up in yours—
not wittily as in his books,
for his laughter never meant to mock you,
but because he believed in

the possibility of a Jewish street
and hoped for redemption in buildings and deeds,
in a street replete with factories—
"Dital," "Dimitrov," "Veber-Kombinat,"

a street which an army of Jewish workers
is drawn to each dawn in distant song.
Only such a street deserves your name—
Oh Master, into deep eternity.

איז ערגעץ וווּ אַזאַ מין האַרבסט פֿאַראַן?

איז ערגעץ וווּ אַזאַ מין האַרבסט פֿאַראַן?
די זון איז פֿאַרגאַן און נישט פֿאַרגאַן;
עס ציט זיך נאָך לאַנג איר זײדענער שלעפּ
אויף מויערן, אויף הײזער, אויף בײמערישע קעפּ.
דו גייסט און דו גייסט און ווייך איז דײַן טראָט —
האָט אויסגעבעט ווער דאָ מיט זײַדנס די שטאָט?
יעדער קלאַנג, יעדער שאַרך ווי נישט זײַן וואָלט פֿון דאַן.
ווּ איז אין האַרבסט אַזאַ אָוונט פֿאַראַן?
ווּ וויגט זיך ווי הי דער צוויציגן־געפֿלעכט
אין סקווערן האַלב טונקל בײַ אָנקום פֿון נעכט?
אין טונקלען ווינקל אַ קעמערל גליק.
אָ, ריר נישט, פֿאַרליר נישט די שטילע מוזיק.
אין בלוי אײַנגעוועבט, אין זײַדנס געניעט,
דורכזיכטיק־ליכטיק דערהויבענע פֿרייד.

92

A Fall Like This Anywhere Else?

Is there a fall like this anywhere else
where the sun has all but set, yet sunset
lingers on stone walls, houses, and tree tops,
meandering, strolling with hushed steps,
as if the city were a silken bed with
every sound, every rustle other-worldly,
until a weave of branches adumbrates a
darkening pattern onto corners of our
small glowing room, and night comes.
Oh, let's not touch, let's not lose the quiet
music woven in blue, sewn in silk—
this luminous, heightened joy.

אָט אַזוי,
ליבע פֿרוי,
זײַ נישט צו שײן:
כ׳האָב נישט ליב די שײן
פֿון מיטן טאָג.
ליבע פֿרוי,
כ׳האָב ליב דעם פֿאַרנאַכט
ווי טרינקען מיט אַ שטרוי קילן ווײַן.
כ׳האָב ליב דעם פֿרימאָרגן
ווען דער טאָג ליגט ווי אַ זאָמען
אין מוטערס בויך פֿאַרבאָרגן
און זאָגט אַזוי פֿיל צו...
כ׳האָב נישט ליב
דעם בלענד
פֿון מיטן טאָג
כ׳האָב ליב ווען דו האַלטסט
מײַן נשמה אין דײַנע הענט
נישט אַזוי אין די הענט
ווי אין די דינע פֿינגער
ס׳פֿאַלן נאָך אַלץ אויף מיר
נאָר ס׳ווערט עפּעס גרינגער

Just Like This

Just like this
dear woman
don't be too beautiful
I don't like the light
at high noon
dearest woman
I like the twilight
like sipping cool wine
through a straw,
I like the dawn
when the day lies like the seed of a life
buried in a mother's belly
and promises so much.
I don't like the glare
of midday
I love it when you hold
my soul in your hands
oh not just in your hands
in your fingers;
the walls still come tumbling down on me
but somehow it becomes easier
lighter.

ניגון...

שפּיל פֿרײַנד,

איך בין דער שאָטן פֿון דעם ניגון דײַנעם.

אויף אַלע וועגן, ווּ עס פֿירט דײַן ליד,

גיי איך ווי אַ שאָטן מיט.

די וועלט, וואָס איך האָב, לייג איך אין דעם ווינקל

נעבן דײַן קלאַוויר,

כ'האָב ליב, ווי מיט דײַן יעדן פֿינגערריר,

מיט יעדן וויברריר,

חרוב ווערט אַ וועלט,

און מיטן צווייטן ריר

וועלט זי אויפֿגעשטעלט,

און פֿון לעבן ביזן טויט, אויף דעם קלײנעם בריק

זאָל רוען מײַן געמיט...

96

Melody

Play on friend—
I am the shadow of your melody.
Onto whatever path your
pain leads, I shadow forth.
This sphere in which I dwell even
lurks in the corner by your piano.
Lovingly I follow the movement of your
fingers and every vibration of the notes.

Although your melody disintegrates
it resurrects in the second movement.
Likewise I hover on that same small bridge
between life and death where my dispirited shadow rests.

אין שטאָט

קראָמען שאָקלען פֿון די שטערנס די שילדן אַראָפּ:
—מיר האַנדלען נישט מער מיט זאַלץ, מיט פֿעפֿער און מיט שניט,
מיט מעל, מיט אײַזן, מיט גלאָזוואַרג און מיט קיט,
מיר האָבן הימל און פֿאַרנאַכטן־גאָלד געזאַמלט, איז אונדז טרעריעריק
דאָס געמיט
און פֿון לבֿנה־שײַן און ווינטן און באַגינענס איז אַ ליד
אין אונדזער אײַנגעווייד אָפּגעשטאָנען...
נײַן, מיר האַנדלען ווײַטער נישט!
מאַכט אונדז צו! מאַכט אונדז צו!

גאַסן וואַרפֿן די מענטשן פֿון זיך אָפּ,
און די טראַמוואַיען און די טאַקסיס און די וועגענער אַראָפּ:
—גענוג געוויזן וועגן! מיר זוכן אַליין אַ וועג!...
ווער זאָגט עס, אַז מיר פֿירן צו פֿאַרשטאָט, צום באַן און צום שפּיטאָל
און צו הײַזער, ווּ עס קינדיגט די וואָג און די שאָל?
מיר וועלן בלאָנדזשען! זיך פֿירן און פֿאַרפֿירן!
און אפֿשר דורך אַ זײַטנוועג צום הימל זיך פֿאַרלירן?...

גאַסן וואַרפֿן די מענטשן פֿון זיך אָפּ...

98

Stores

Stars shake night down over the foreheads of the stores;
no longer do they deal in flour, in vegetables and grains,
in glassware, window panes and putty;
again twilight mirrors our own sad spirits,
the viscera of our very being, which we had suppressed
from dawn 'til dark—now it closes us! closes us!

Streets cast their people aside,
their buses and taxis and wagons;
—who says you can still ride to suburban hospitals
or houses where the scales of justice still weigh in?

We and we alone lead ourselves astray, lose our way
on side roads enroute to the sky.

Streets cast their people aside.

מײַן גאָט! איך וויל אויסגיין אין דיר,
ווי עס גייט דאָס גרעזל אויס אין האַרבסט
אין דיר,
ווי עס ציט זיך דער ניגון אויס פֿאַרחלשט
ביז זײַן סוף
צו דיר
און ווערט שטילער, שטילער,
דיך דערזעענדיק.
ווי עס גייט דער טאָג אויס אויף די ראַנדן —
צו דיר.
און ווי דער ווינט,
וואָס זוכט דאָך קיינעם נישט אויף זײַן וועג,
נאָר דיך,
אין דיר פֿאַרפֿאַלן צו ווערן!
ווי דער ים, וואָס די גאַנצע וועלט איז אים ענג

100

Untitled

God of mine!
With my last breath
I shall become one with you,
as in autumn a tiny blade of grass
dies into you;
as melody's end stretches
ever more faintly
unto you,
quieter and quieter
as it reaches you;
or as day fades to the edge—
of you
or the wind's path seeks no one
but you
to become lost within!
And how the ocean's
love for you
causes all of earth to be crowded together
by water's years already
of dashing wildly about
at a loss to find you!

אויפֿן אומשלאַגפּלאַץ

אויפֿן אומשלאַגפּלאַץ נישטאָ ערשט קיינער, קיינער,
פֿאַר וואָס איז שטיל? זאָלן ווינטן זיך צעברויזן,
זאָלן צום הימל זיך בײַלן אַצינד די פֿויסטן
פֿון טרערנקוואַל זאָלן שלײדערן זיך טרערן.

אויפֿן אומשלאַגפּלאַץ שטייסט ערשט איינער, איינער,
וואָלסט די זון פֿאַר כּעס ערשט אויסגעלאָשן.
שרײַען ווילסטו, נאָר ס׳איז שטום דײַן לשון.
טו אויס די שיך, דו טרעטסט דאָ אויף געוויינען.

טו אויס די שיך, הייליק איז די ערד דאָ,
געווייקט אין פּײַן פֿון קינדערשע נשמות,
און יעדער וואַנט — אַ כּותל־המערבֿי.

איך בין קיין העלד און בין נישט קיין נבֿיא,
נאָר כ׳שטיק די זון בײַם האַלדז, ביז זי שווערט דאָ
זיך אַליין צעפֿליקן פֿאַר נקמה.

102

Umschlagplatz in Warsaw

On Umschlagplatz there is no one now, no one.
WHY is it so quiet? May winds whip up in anger,
may fist-clenching at the sky now bring forth
tears from the source of all tears!

On Umschlagplatz I stand alone now, alone.
In my anger I would extinguish the sun!
I want to shout, "Remove your shoes!
You are stepping on crying!" But I'm mute.

Remove your shoes; the ground is holy here.
Soaked with the anguish of children's souls,
every wall is a wailing wall!

I who am neither hero nor prophet,
would throttle the sun until it hereby swears
to rip itself to shreds for revenge!

טאַנגאָ

דו האַלטסט איר אין די אָרעמס, נאָר זי איז אַוועק...
דרייען זיך ווי בלעטער נעכט און טעג
האַרבסטיק אַזוי, אָוונטיק אַזוי.

איז מאַלע וואָס סע טרעפֿט? איז וואָס זשע דען דער מער?
לאָזט דאָס פֿידעלע אַזוי נאַריש טרער נאָך טרער
ווי אַ פֿאַרבלאָנדזשעט קינד.

די מאַמע זאָגט: איך גיי! איך קום! אָט אָ בין איך דאָ!
נאָר ס׳וויינט אָפּ דאָס קינד דערפֿאַר אַ גאַנצע שעה,
ווייל ס׳איז די מאַמע נישט געווען.

ס׳וועט זײַן גוט, פֿילסט עס נישט בחוש?
צי טויט צי לעבן וועט געבן דיר אַ קוש,
וועט אַלץ איינס זײַן גוט.

104

Tango

You hold her in your arms but she is gone…
night and day twirl like leaves of a tree
autumn-like, evening-like, and we—

but who cares what happens? What's the problem?
the little violin foolishly sheds tear after tear
like a lost child in fear

whose mother says: I go! I come! Here I am!
but the child cries a whole hour there
because the mother wasn't anywhere…

things will be all right either way—
don't you sense that whether it's death
or life that gives you a kiss, things will be okay.

דעם פֿרעמדן מענטש

מיר קאָנען זיך נישט, נאָר ווי פֿאַרשטענדלעך פּראָסט
דו צינדסט אין פֿײַער מײַנעם אָן דײַן פּאַפּיראָס,

נאָר עפּעס וועקט זיך, עפּעס אָנט מײַן ווײַטער זעקסטער חוש —
ס'האָבן זיך פּאַפּיראָסן צוויי אַ פֿראָסטן טאָג געקושט.

און ווי קלאָר ווי דער שֹכל זאָגט: מיר דאַרפֿן זײַן זיך פֿרעמד —
האָט טיף אין אונדז זיך עפּעס וואָס פֿאַרשעמט

און ברעכט אויף אַלע צוימען פֿון פֿאַרשטאַנד
און נאָענט מיר ווערן ווי פֿון לאַנג באַקאַנט.

Strangers

We don't know each other, but how simply
you ignite your cigarette with mine

and my suppressed sixth sense stirs—
as on this ordinary day our two cigarettes kiss.

My rational mind says we should remain strangers—
despite this shameful conflict burning within me

but at last my defenses break through their fences
and we become intimates, as if we'd known each other forever.

אין דאָרף

אָ, פּשוט פֿאָלק פֿון דאָרפֿיש־קלײנער גאַס,
כ'בין ביז בלוט פֿאַרליבט אין אײַער שטײַגער.
איך קנײַפ װי איר דאָס ברויט און פֿאַרטרינק מיט קװאַס,
קוק אויבן אויף דער זון און װער געװױר דעם זײַגער.

װי איר, כ'האָב ליב צו רעדן הויך
און לאַכן אויפֿן קול אַ פֿרײַלעכן געלעכטער,
אויב לאַכן — איז זיך האַלטן פֿאַרן בויך —
און עס לאַכן מיט אין כאָר אַלע זין און טעכטער.

אװעקשטעלן אין מיטן טיש דעם בראָשט װי צונטער רויט,
פֿון האַלץ די לעפֿל װײגן זיך װי װעסלעס,
און װי בּאָרשט — די באַקן בײַ דער מויד,
װען מאַמע מיט די שבֿחים לכֿבֿוד איר פֿאַרגעסט זיך.

און מע כאַפּט אַ טאַנץ און מע זינגט אַ ליד,
און מע פֿאַרט דערנאָך אויף דער אײַנגעשפּאַנטער דראָזשקע —
און װײסט נישט, צי איז עס פֿרײַד, צי װײנט נאָר אין דער מיט
מיטן האַרבסט צוזאַמען בײַם יינגל די האַרמאָשקע.

In the Village

Oh simple people of small village streets
I love your customs; they are in my blood.
I too pinch off a bit of bread and drink kvass.

I too like to talk and laugh loudly when happy
so that just like all your sons and daughter
I join in when you are belly-laughing.

In the middle of the table the wooden spoons
row like oars in the fire red borscht—and just
like borscht are the young woman's cheeks
when the father forgets himself with praise.

They dance a little, sing a song, and afterwards
crowd into a droshke and don't even know
or care if the youth playing the harmonica
is mixing summer joy with autumnal crying.

Notes to Section II

"Chinese Man": Sen=wood, group of trees, Yun= mist, Tang=common family name, Peking=Beijing.

The Sino-Japanese War began in earnest in 1937 after at least six years of more isolated military actions. In 1936 the Japanese claimed the Chinese blew up the Marco Polo rail bridge 30 miles north of Beijing (Peking). This became their rationale for the invasion. Although Beijing itself was not destroyed, many fled. Nanking, then the Capital, was moved twice... Until 1936 the USSR did not have a "united front policy" toward the Sino-Japanese War. But in 1937 Chiang-Kai Shek, who had been concentrating on fighting a civil war with the Chinese Communists, was forced by his Manchurian general to collaborate with the Chinese communists in a united front against the Japanese. Prior to this time the Soviets had the same policy toward Chiang-Kai-Shek as toward Hitler (See 1939 Soviet-Hitler Pact). Therefore, this poem, dated 1938, and written and published in Russia in 1940, surely reflects Emiot's awareness of the shift in Soviet policy, although he may have begun the poem prior to the policy shift. (I am indebted to Chinese scholar Professor Charless Wivell, of the University of Rochester's linguistics depart ment, for providing the information in this footnote.)

"On Seeing La Gioconda": La Gioconda is the actual name of the woman known as Mona Lisa, painted by Leonardo di Vinci between 1503-1506. However, it is also the name of an Italian opera by Amilcare Pouchielli, composed between 1839-1861, whose third act, second scene, is a well-known ballet. Thus Emiot's poem refers to both—a kind of synesthetic melding of a visual, an auditory, and a mythic image.

"Tamara Hanum": Dance has a long, important, multi-varied history in Uzbekistan. It is spectacular, lyrical, and passionate. Tamara Hanum renovated the art of dancing in the first half of the twentieth century and was a beautiful and famous singer and dancer whom Emiot saw in performance.

"prayers for the dead": Kol Nidre

"final prayer of atonement": Niele

"My Premonition of a Lullaby": "You wonderful person, you." — This final line of the poem is written in Russian.

"Before Spring": "Elder": The Yiddish word for "old man" and "mistake" are the same.

"Sholem Aleykem Street": Sholem Aleykem was a great, famous, and beloved Yiddish writer who immortalized the common folk, (1859-1916). *The Tevye Stories,* upon which *Fiddler on the Roof* is based, are examples of his humor and common touch. He is sometimes referred to as the Mark Twain of Yiddish literature. The main street in the capitol of Birobidjhan, the First Autonomous Soviet Jewish Republic, is named for him. In this republic it was hoped that Jews could at last be first class citizens, allowed to own land, farm, and have access to all occupations. The republic was originally founded, instrumentally, by Stalin. Later many of its citizens were liquidated as "internationalists" or "bourgeois enemies" of the people. Emiot was sent there in 1944, as a journalist by the Russian Joint Anti-Fascist Committee, which later became an international organization to help Russia defeat Hitler. In 1948 he was sent to a Soviet prison, where he remained for seven years of a ten year sentence until the Khrushchev era.

"Stores": See folksong, "Der Kremer," about an impoverished storekeeper. Different versions of this poem exist.

In Yiddish the word for "star" and "forehead" is the same.

"Untitled" ("God of mine!..."): The original poem was written in Chasidic dudele form.

"Umschlagplatz in Warsaw": Umschlag: Yiddish—hit/strike; German: many meanings—merchandize junction redirection center, railroads, also envelop, etc. Polish: A marked spot now, with a memorial, where Jews were boarded to be sent to Treblinka.

"Remove your shoes": Orthodox Jews wear slippers in mourning.

"rip itself to shreds": Orthodox Jews "sit shiva" in mourning for seven days. This ritual includes the renting of one's clothing.

"In the Village": This was originally number three in the Siberian cycle.

Droshke: a crude but sturdy wooden cart used for transportation and cartage in the shtetl, usually with a horse and driver.

Section III

1958–1963

Poland, United States

In Melody Absorbed, Covered Mirrors, In Middle Years

AFTER THE PUBLICATION of *Yearning*, in 1957 in Poland, Emiot made his way to the United States in 1958, after being assisted by various refugee organizations in relocating his family who had moved to Rochester, New York and lost track of him. Although traumatized and in frail health, he was invited to be the Writer in Residence at the local Jewish Community Center. His tasks included publishing a tri-lingual literary journal in English, Yiddish and Hebrew called *Jewish Roots*, giving lectures, and of course writing. It was touted as the first such position in the country. How this position came about is not clear, nor if or what it paid. It did involve annual employee evaluations. Gradually Emiot also became involved in the Rochester literary community, where he enjoyed friendships, literary recognition, respect, and periodic help, in salon-like atmospheres, and where he in turn shared his considerable knowledge of European literature. Robert Koch, then a dean at the University of Rochester, was one of his most stalwart friends. Attempts at translation were made by both writers and lay members of the Jewish community. Much of Emiot's creative and limited physical energy was focused on recovering, remembering, or rewriting both poetry and prose from his previous work. He also began to write his prose memoir about the Gulag. New poems began to emerge as well. All these efforts of recall and reorganization document how well he remembered his lost work and how carefully it had been constructed.

In Melody Absorbed, the first of these books published, in Yiddish, in Rochester, contains his Siberia and his Lublin poems as well as others. A discussion of his time in Siberia is in Section IV.

The Lublin Poems: Emiot wrote this cycle of poems in 1957, or shortly thereafter, in transit to Warsaw after seven years of a ten-year sentence to a Gulag for crimes of "internationalism" during Stalin's most infamous reign of terror against Jews. But the Lublin poems were first published in 1961 in the USA. It was understandable that he would have yearned to visit Lublin after the Gulag, given its large and historic Jewish presence, and its renown Yeshiva, currently part of the touristic "Chasidic Trail." Known as the School of the Wise Men of Lublin, the Yeshiva was erected in 1930 as the largest in the world. The old Jewish cemetery in town dated from the sixteenth century.

(Emiot had studied for the rabbinate at another distinguished Yeshiva in his youth.) The poems are infused with reverence, nostalgia, evident learnedness, and sorrow. Equally present are personal anguish, loneliness and hints of secularity. The struggle between these modes creates poetic tension. However, Emiot used two earlier poems to start the Lublin cycle: The first, written in 1938, honors the major poet Jacob Glatstein, who was born in Lublin but also became famous in the United States. The second earlier poem, written in 1932, is about his father's death. He was twenty-three when he wrote it and about forty-six when he finished the Lublin cycle. By then many of the famous gravestones Emiot refers to in the poems had been ripped up and used by the Nazis in the construction of the visibly nearby, grisly, Maidanek Death Camp.

Originally the bulk of these poems were written in rhymed Petrarchan sonnet form, a favorite form of Emiot's in which he was very skilled. The actual sequence of the poems is both curious and understandable: They begin with the mystery of death, eulogize both his biological and an important literary father, and vividly and extensively describe Lublin itself, pre and post war. They are highly evocative of the city, historically laden, and replete with both Jewish and Christian life in Lublin. They are tender but bitter, reverential but cynical. I am indebted to Magda Pokrzycka-Walczak, whom I met in Lublin, for assistance with the historical aspects of these poems as well as emotional generosity. A journalist and Christian, she had been affectionately dubbed a granddaughter by elderly remnants of the Jewish community. Emiot refers to the "haunting hum, thin as a dove," the soulful wedding tunes of klezmers, and finally is drawn to the humming of a Viennese waltz by the provocative gentile pharmacist he encounters. In the Lublin poems per se there are relatively minimal but still telling references to the constant presence of music in Emiot's metaphorical life.

However, in the book *In Melody Absorbed* itself, there are significant poems about music. "Prayer to Bach in a Minor Key," actually pleads with the composer Bach that "his melody reach out and find me" and make him when dead worthy of God's grace "like the littlest leaf on a tree." Obviously Emiot, who in growing up in an orthodox household was not close to Bach's music, had come to see its intrinsically spiritual power and genius. So he prays in this poem not to God himself but to Bach! The long, wide-ranging title poem of the collection, *In Melody Absorbed* is dedicated to a musicologist named Israel Rabinowich. In this poem he prays directly to God, inspired by music to wish for a decent remaining life and death. His persuasions range through childhood memories, and a special, famous lullaby, which is not included, that promises but never made good on its promises of a life full of "raisins and almonds." Clearly Emiot's opus is more concerned with his inner life than events in the larger society.....perhaps the inevitable aftermath of his difficult and diverse life. Yet, the poem "Perfume" affirms hope despite everything, straddling the polarities of the former two poems, speaking of the song of flowers in an extended metaphor likening it to the lingering aroma of white wine, and to memories of love, grief, and the past years "scattered like coins." Surely the most striking aspect of this quasi-musical metaphor is the coupling together synesthetically of song and smell in the context of time.

In *Covered Mirrors,* compiled in Yiddish in Rochester in 1962, Emiot continues his efforts to reconstruct his oeuvre and adds to it. However, all three of the books in Section III contain prose and translations in addition to poetry. In particular, *Covered Mirrors* was published in Buenos Aires.

In Middle Years, his Yiddish publication in 1963, in Rochester, has a number of striking poems. The prize-winning poem "Let's Detain the Summer" mixes imagery of the passing of summer with imagery from his Gulag days, speaking of enticing summer "into the deep valleys—the world's love wounds." The poem titled "The Violin" is about a quarrel between a violin and a bass. While it is an extended musical analogy, and a bit tongue in cheek, it is obviously about a human drama as well. A poem titled "Jazz" is Emiot's first and only attempt to use that medium in a poem. It is not easy to place it in his life story; perhaps it refers to his youthful days in Warsaw. In contrast, the poem called "To Someone" probably comes from the period after Moscow, and after his earlier poem on the tango. Just as it laments the passage of all the good things in life, his poem called "Vivaldi" does the same, asking "what are years? Where are my years?" Finally, Emiot writes a fierce and fear-ridden poem about the sonnet form itself, "running at the edge of the earth."

אַ מילב וואָס שטאַרבט

אַ מילב וואָס שטאַרבט אין אַ נאַרע פֿון אַן אַלטן בוך
איז איר אויך אַ שׂאָ די וועלט...

טרעפֿט: אַ מענטש מישט בלעטער אויף אַ מאָל,
גיט די זון אַ שײַן אין אַ מילבנשפּאַלט,
גייט די מילב דער זון אַנטקעגן,
זאָגט די מילב: ווײַזט אויס ס׳איז פֿרילינג הײַנט,
נאָר מײַנע לונגען האָט שוין אויפֿגעפֿרעסן
די ווײַלגאָטנע וואַנט, דער קאַלטער אַכזר,
סע קומט דער זומער אויף דער וועלט
און איך גיי שטאַרבן.

הייבט די מילב די אויגן מיט געבעט:

— אָ, גאָט, מײַן שפּאַן איז אַזוי קורץ,
און גייט נישט ווײַטער פֿונעם בלאָט אין בוך,
כ׳בין דאָס גאָנצע לעבן שטיל געווען און נישט געגלוסט קיין פֿרעמדס,
און נישט מקנא געווען קיין מאָל די פֿליג,
דעם אומרו וואָס זיצט נישט אויף קיין אָרט,
און נישט דעם מענטש, וואָס איך באַגרײַף שוין נישט.
לאָז מיך אונטערלעבן כאָטש נאָר אַ טאָג, צי צוויי,
כ׳האָב אַזוי מורא פֿאַרן סוד פֿון טויט
צו בלײַבן שווײַיגנדיק ווי מײַן טאַטע ליגן,
כ׳וועק אים אַלע אינדערפֿרי: טאַטע, ס׳איז שוין טאָג,
און ער איז שטום און גיט זיך נישט קיין ריר.

A Mite That Dies

A mite that dies in the lair of an old book
also misses the world…

It happens: Suddenly a person turns the pages,
sun shines in a crack,
the mite crawls toward it
sensing today it appears to be spring
although his lungs have already been devoured
by the damp brutal cold—
summer is coming to the world
yet he's going to die.

The mite lifts his eyes in prayer:

> "Oh God, my stride is so short,
> I can't go further than this page;
> I've been quiet all my days,
> not coveting another's life
> not even envious of the fly—
> of restless creatures who aren't in one place
> or all those inexplicably busy humans."

Please let me live a little more, at least another day or two;
I am so afraid of the mystery of death,
of lying as silently as my father
whom I try to wake each morning:

> Father, it is already day I say,

but he is mute and does not move.

אַלט־לובלין

יעקבֿ גלאַטשטײן — דעם לובלינער.

וואָס איז פֿאַרט אַזוינס וואָס שמידט צו זיך מײַן בליק,
קוריט און קוריט און גראַטעס און צעבראָכענער שטיין,
מײַן אָרעם פֿאָלק, דײַן עבֿר — פֿול געוויין
פֿלאַצן פֿון יעדן פֿון שטיין אַרויס, ווי פֿון אַ האַלדז דערשטיקט.

געסלעך, שמוץ, געשטאַנק און קלעפֿיקייט, גענוג,
גענוג געזען דעם פֿײַן. איך וויל
דאָ פֿון די געסלעך אַרויס, נאָר שטיל
רופֿט אַ קול ווי אַ טויבנשטים: צוריק!

אָ, אַלט־לובלין, אַנטלויף איך דען פֿון דיר? דו יאָגסט מיר נאָך,
און אין מײַן צימער הער איך נאָך דײַן בראָך,
דורות ווייטיק, שאַנד און פֿײַן.

צי קען איך דען אַנטלויפֿן, אַז אין מײַן בלוט
ברומט דער ניגון, דער זעלביקער, דאָס ליד
וואָס פֿילט דײַנע געסלעך אָן מיט אַזאַ פֿאַרכטיקן געוויין.

120

The Lublin Poems: Old Lublin

for Jacob Glatstein—the poet from Lublin

What is so riveting that I can't avert my eyes?
Is it the dirt, rubble, barred windows and broken gravestones
of my poor people's lament-filled past bursting
from every stone like cries from a strangled throat?

Of small grungy streets, foul odors and contagiousness
I've had enough, enough! I have long witnessed this anguish
and wished to flee these narrow alley ways
that as insidiously as a dove's voice entice me:

                                    Back!

Oh old Lublin even if I run away you pursue me;
within my room I still hear the disastrous generations—
the ancient anguish of pain and shame.

How can I ever flee when in my very own veins
flows the same mournful melody, the exact same one, the saddest
of songs that fills your dear little streets with such dreadful lament!

ווי אַן איבעגעקערטער אינגעווייד, ראָפֿיק שוין אין בראַנד,
ליגסטו, געטאָ ייִדישער, צופֿוסנס פֿון לובלין,
פֿאַרשטאָט קראָקעווער ווייס נישט וואָס מיט דיר צו טון,
איז אַזוי פֿיל אָרעמקייט נאָך דאָ אין גאַנצן לאַנד?

ביסטו אײַנגענייט אויף פֿלייצע אירער — אַ לאַטע פֿון דער שאַנד,
אַ קיִן־צייכן לאָז זי טראָגן פֿון דײַן שוואַרץ גזר־דין,
ווונדערלעך, ווי אומעטום, גייט אויך דאָ אויף דער באַגין,
נאָר איבער דיר פֿירן וואָלקנס אייביק אַ שוואַרצן בר־מינן.

מעגסט שוין דורכגיין הײַנט דעם ברייטן ייִדן־טויער,
נאָר דיר איז ליב נאָך אַלץ דער פֿאַרשפֿאַרטער טרויער,
אַ דערמאָנונג בלײַבט ער אייביק, אַ פֿאַראַכטונג פֿאַרן פֿײַנד.

אויף יאַטעטשנע גאַס איז אייביק ווי צו נעילה,
דעם מהרש״ל־שולס קלײַנע פֿענצטער — ווי אויגן בײַ אַ תּפֿילה
צום הימל אויפֿגעהויבן, בעטנדיק פֿאַרוויינט.

The Lublin Poems: Untitled #2

Like an eviscerated gut churning in pickled brine
the Jewish ghetto lies at the foot of Lublin...
not even Krakow's poorest slum compares—
is it possible such poverty still exists in the country!

Are you a patch of shame sewn on Lublin's shoulder?
The mark of Cain's black fate you must bear?
Remarkably dawn still comes—
but the clouds carry a black corpse!

Today I can enter the wide Jewish gate,
although still caged by grief, it reminds me
forever of my outrage at the enemy.

On Yatechoveh Street it is forever the Ne'ilah time
and in the small windows of the Maharoshe Synagogue
weeping eyes in prayer implore the heavens.

סע פֿירן אַלץ נאָך בוידן אין דער ייִדן־גאַס, פֿון לענדער פֿיר געקומען

אויף די גאַסן האָבן מיך פרנסים אַזוי טרויעריקלעך אָנטפֿאַנגען,

און סע גייט דער שמועס וועגן פדיון־שבֿויים, מ׳האָט ייִדן וווּ
געפֿאַנגען,

און סע גייט דער שמועס איבער גזרות וואָס לויערן און קומען.

ס׳איז אַזש קראַנק מיַין קאָפּ, כ׳האָב אַזוי פֿיל צער ערשט דאָ פֿאַרנומען,

איז עמעץ נאָך אַ באַלבירער אין דער נאָענט געגאַנגען,

משה מונטאַלטו וועט אַ רפֿואה מיר דערלאַנגען,

ס׳איז פֿון וויַיטיק פֿאַרטריקנט מיר דער גומען.

אָ, אַלט־לובלין, ס׳וועלן זיך נאָך יאָרן אַזוי ציִען דיַינע געשפּענסטער,

און כאַטש ערגעץ זינגט שוין דאָ אַרויס אַ ראַדיאָ פֿון אַ פֿענצטער

אַ פֿלאָכן טאַנגאָ, און סע זשומען איבער דיר אויך עראָפּלאַנען,

וועט אייביק אין דער שקיעה פֿאַרן גאָניטן אויער

זיך טראָגן פֿון אונטער יאָרן לאַסט — ס׳געוויין פֿון דורות, טרויער,

און יענע טונקעלע שרעק, נישט פֿון דאַנען.

The Lublin Poems: Untitled #3

Covered wagons rumble through the streets bringing Jews,
captured prisoners from other lands, refugees whom the leaders
of our community greet sorrowfully, whispering of ransom,
but hinting of lurking, evil decrees that surely will come.

My head is just so sick; grief overwhelms me.
Someone is just walking by, Moshe Montalto so it seems
but could he, could even he give me any real remedy
for my palate by now so parched with pain?

Oh, old Lublin, this specter will haunt me all my years,
even though from some window above I can hear a radio playing
the music of a flat tango and overhead the droning of airplanes.

But forever in the sunset for my practiced ear
will be carried the burden of these years of
grief and dark fear coming from elsewhere.

אַ פֿרימאָרגן אין בית־מדרשל פֿון "חוזה מלובלין",
אַ בעקער שטייט בײַם עמוד און יאָגט שנעל־שנעל צום מנין,
בעלי־מלאָכות און סוחרימלעך וואָס יאָגן זיך צו קנין...
ווּ לויפֿסטו, האַרץ מײַנס, פֿון דאַנען, ווּהין?

דיך יאָגט די ווירקלעכקייט און ס׳איז דיר ליבער דער רוִין,
פֿון אונטער חורבֿות זעסטו אָט די אַלע הייליקע געשטאַלטן,
אין די ווינקלען דאָ אין איטלעכן זײנען זיי באַהאַלטן,
און דאָס ברומען זייערס — ווי אַ טויב אַזוי נאָגנדיק דין!

ס׳האָט אָפּגעדאַווּנט דאָס געזעמל קרעמערס, זיי זײנען שוין
פֿאַרשוווּנדן,
און אַ פֿלאַם אַזאַ האָט פּלוצעם העל זיך אָנגעצונדן,
אַזאַ פֿאַרכטיקע, אַזאַ איבערמענטשלעכע פֿרייד דאָ.

דער "חוזה מלובלין" און די הייליקע חבֿריא
און סע גליט דער פֿלאַם פֿון די תּלמידים, די געטרײַע,
אָט באַלד הערסטו דאָס קול פֿון ייִד־הקדוש, דײַן גרויסן זיידן.

The Lublin Poems: Untitled #4

This morning in the small synagogue of the Prophet of Lublin
an ordinary baker stands at the pulpit and speaks quickly, too quickly
to the minyan of craftsmen and small merchants eager for spiritual property...
Where are you running, heart of mine, from here to where?

Reality chases you but still you prefer the ruins
from beneath which, hidden in each and every corner,
you imagine coming forth holy images and hear
emanating their haunting hum, thin as a dove's.

The clatch of shopkeepers have finished praying
and by now dispersed like a sudden flame,
a fearsome yet awesome burst of super-human joy...

That Prophet of Lublin among his crowd of disciples,
the flame of his faithful pupils glowing, his voice recalled—
the voice of that Holy Jew, your spiritual great grandfather.

ווו איז די זון פֿאַראַן, איז ערגעץ דאָ אַ שטראַל
פֿאַר אַלע קעלערן פֿינכטע, וואָס זיינען דאָ פֿאַרבליבן?
יונגע אַרבעטער זינגען פֿון פֿרילינג און פֿון ליבן,
נאָר דער "כּל־נדרי" וויינט אַרויס פֿון "אינטערנאַציאָנאַל".

און סע גייט נאָך אַלץ אַרום געבויגן דער מהרש״ל,
ער האָט נאָר וואָס דעם עולם פֿון די געסלעך פֿאַרטריבן,
ווי דער פּסוק זאָגט: גיי, מײַן פֿאָלק, אין די שטיבן,
וואַרט ביז דער צאָרן מײַדט, דעם פֿײַנדס אָנפֿאַל.

און אַלע גלאָקן קלינגען אויס דעם זעלביקן באַטײַט,
פֿון אַלע עקן שטראָמען פֿאַרכטיק־פֿרומע לײַט,
באַלד וועט אַ ייִדס גוף זיך קאַרטשען אין די פֿלאַמען.

הער, הער, דער וויינט אין נאָענטן הויף
אַן עלילת־דם, חלילה, אָדער אַ "שילער־געלויף",
אָדער גאָר זיי ביידע צוזאַמען.

128

The Lublin Poems: Untitled #5

Where is the sun, is there even a ray somewhere
for all the damp cellars remaining—
oh for sure the young workers sing of spring and love,
but Kol Nidre sobs out of the International.

And the Marharoshe walks about stooped over,
dispersing the crowd from the street,
for as the Bible says, "Go my people into the houses
and wait until the enemy's wraith wanes."

And all the bells ring out with the same warning
as the pious flee from the fearsome evils,
but soon a Jew's body will writhe in flames.

Listen, listen the wind in the nearby courtyard
is a Blood Accusation, or a mob of rioting students
run amok—or both together.

וואָלאַכן טרוויעריקע פֿון אַלטייִדישע כלי־זמרים,
נאָך נאָגט אין האַרץ ביז געוווייַן דער טרוויעריקער ניגון:
הונדערט יאָרן שוין אַנטשוויגן, און דאָך נישט אַנטשוויגן,
פֿון יעדן שפֿאַלט, פֿון יעדן וואָנט — צו הערן קלאָר אים.

אָ, פֿאַעט פֿון יענער צייַט, איך גיי אום ביי דייַן אָרעם,
פֿון פֿאַרלאַנגען ווילד גענאָגט, פֿון ווייַטיק באַזיגן,
נאָר פֿון די געסלעך דאָ פֿירן אונדז די שטיגן
צום ווייַטן, אומבאַקאַנטן טורעם.

אָ, וועמען דען דעם צער פֿאַרטרויען, די ליבשאַפֿט צו פֿאַרהיטן?
ס׳זייַנען אַזוי אומעטיק דייַנע שטילינקע פֿיוטים,
און ס׳איז פֿול אין זיי דער דעמער אין די שטערן.

אָ, האַרץ, פֿאַרליבט־אַנטוישט, אין בלעטער פֿון סידורים
פֿאַרטויישט אויף תּחינות־קינות, אָ, יסורים
דיכטערישע, באַפֿייכט מיט תּפֿילהדיקע טרערן.

The Lublin Poems: Untitled #6

Sad wedding music by old Jewish klezmers—
your soulful tunes gnaw at the heart until I cry
for the one hundred years already silent and yet not silent—
still clearly sounding from every crevice and crack.

Oh, poet of that time, I follow at your elbow
wildly gnawed by desire and hopelessly flawed by pain
through the narrow byway whose stairs
lead to the distant unknown towers.

Oh, to whom shall I confide this grief, or how to abort this love?
Psalms so sad, so endearingly quiet,
you are full of the twilight of the stars.

Oh, heart in love, disillusioned by the pages of prayer books
already exchanged for tales of lamentation on Tishev B'Ov—
oh, agony of poetry stained with tears of prayer.

עס איז אומעטום זײַן גײַסט פֿאַראַן פֿאַרכטיק־פֿרום בצניעות,
און די שטראָפֿרייד זײַנע צום רמ״א פֿאַר לערנען גאָר חקירה:
"איידער אזַא אַהבֿה איז שוין גלײַכער דאָך מיראה" —
די זונליכט זעט זיך דורך װי דורך צוגעלעגנטע װײַעס.

איך בין אַליין אַצינד, נאָר אַ גערויש װי װיקלען פֿון רצועות,
די שכינה האָט זיך געשײדט מיט דער װעלט, זיך אויסגעװײַלט
איר דירה,
דאָס שאָרכן עס אין דער הייך די װײַסע פֿליגלען אירע,
און זויגט דאָ פֿון דער שטילקייט טיף איר חיות.

איך װאָלט שװוערן: כ'בין געװוען שוין דאָ װען מיט הונדערט יאָר
צוריק,
װײַל ס'איז אַזוי באַקאַנט מיר אַלץ, דער װײַטיקלעכער גליק,
װאָס רוישט װי אַלטער װײַן אין אַן אונטערערדישן קעלטער.

כ'האָב מיט אַלע דורות דאָ געלעבט, װאָס זײַנען שוין פֿאַרגאַנגען,
ס'איז אַלץ דאָ אַלט יאָרהונדערט, שוין גאָרנישע צו דערמאָנען,
נאָר מײַן זעל איז עלטער, עלטער, עלטער!

The Lublin Poems: In Maharoshe Synagogue

His spirit is everywhere, fearsomely pious but virtuously modest
and his reproof to the Rama for studying speculation, of all things
is that "fear is preferable to such Divine Love"—
because sunlight can filter through even half-closed eyelashes…

I am alone now, except for a faint noise—as if from the winding
of the leather straps of my phylacteries—for a divine manifestation
has parted from the world, chosen this dwelling, rustles its white wings
restlessly on high, and sucks from the deep silence delight-filled vitality.

I could swear I was here a hundred years ago—
everything is so familiar, this painful happiness
that gurgles like old wine in an underground cellar.

I have lived here with all the generations that have passed away…
everything is hundreds of years old, and beyond recall,
but oh my soul is older, older, older.

אונטן דאָרט וויינט דער בית־הקבֿרות־שמשׂ, אַ כּאַטקעלע ווי קליין,
און אינעווייניק ליגט אונטער אַ פֿערענע אָן זיך דער קבֿרות־מאַן
    קראַנק,
ס׳האָט דער בית־הקבֿרות־טויער קיין מת נישט אָנגעקוקט שוין לאַנג,
און אַ פּרוטה פֿון אַ גאַסט שוין לאַנגע טעג נישט אָנגעזען.

ליגט ער, הוסט ער, ער האָט אַ מעבֿר־יבוק אין ספֿרים־שרענקל שטיין,
ער וואָלט די קבֿרים וויזן פֿאַר אַ קליין אַ געשאַנק,
נאָר מאַך, אַז ס׳זיצענען זײַנע פֿיס שוין בלאָ געשוואָלן, קראַנק,
און באַוויזן כאַטש מיט אַ נס אויפֿן באַרג צו גיין.

שיקט ער מיט זײַן אייניקל, אַ יִינגעלע דרײַצן יאָר שוין אַלט,
ער ווייס פֿון מהר״ם, ר׳ שכנא און מהרש״ל,
און אַלע קדושים־קבֿרים — אַ פֿירער אין דער נויט!

ער ווייס אויך די פֿרנסים־שורה קלאָר און פֿלינק צו וויזן,
און געדענקט דעם זיידנס אַלע דאָטעגרײַזן,
— ר׳ ייִד, גיט אויף אַ שטיקל ברויט!

The Lublin Poems: Untitled #8

The keeper of this cemetery lives in a tiny hut down slope,
except now he lies on a coverless featherbed, sick
for so long that the cemetery gate has not lately seen a corpse,
nor has he earned a zloty from a visitor in many days.

He just lies there and coughs, beside the Yabbok Book in his bookcase...
if he could he would guide me through the graveyard for a small gratuity,
but what can I expect when his legs are so swollen and blue
that he can barely crawl up and down the slopes?

Instead he sends his grandson, who although only thirteen
already knows the location of the gravesites of the Maharam and Maharshal
and all the other holy men—a guide indeed in a time of need.

He also knows to point out the names of the other community leaders
and remembers all his grandfather's mistaken dates, which he intersperses
    with begging—
        Mr. Jew, Sir, give me a coin for a piece of bread!

אַלטער בית־החיים

אַ, דורות פּיַן אין באַרג פֿאַרקוועטשט, אַ, שפּיציקער געשטווייר,
פֿון בלוט און אײַטער האַרט, אַלט בית־עולם אין לובלין,
ס׳לייגט דער פֿרילינג פֿלאַסטערלעך, גרעזעלעך פֿון גרין,
נאָר דער געשטווייר ווערט האַרטער נאָך, אַט זיצט ער שוין בײַ מיר.

בין איך ווילד פֿון ווייַ, פֿאַרבלאָנדזשע איך צו אַ טיר,
אַפּטייק. די אַפּטייקערין אין ווײַסן אַנגעטון
שמינקט די ליפּן זיך און ברומט אַ וואַלס פֿון ווײַן,
"ס׳וועט פֿאָגאָדע זײַן?" — אַ ראַנדעווו בײַ איר!

— אַוודאי אַ גאַסט, אַ טוריסט, האָב איך וואָס געזען?
דאָס הויז פֿון ווינצענטי פֿאָל וואָס שטייט שוין דאַ זיבעט וועץ
דאָס טײַער קראָקעווער פֿון גאָר אַ ווײַטן דור?

פֿון יאָרהונדערט, אַ, שטאָט! נאָר ס׳איז פֿרילינג אין לובלין,
די אַפּטייקערין ברומט אַ וואַלס פֿון ווײַן
און גלוקט אין שפּיגעלע זיך די בלאָנדע האָר.

The Lublin Poems: Old Jewish Cemetery

Oh, generations of compressed anguish, these thrusted mounds
of blood and hardened pus in Lublin's cemetery
spring now patches with small compresses of green grasses
near whose ever-hardening heaps I sit and weep

wild with pain until I lose my way to a drugstore
where a white coated pharmacist is applying lipstick
humming a Viennese waltz, and asks "if there will be weather"—
then proposes a rendezvous at her place,

teasing of course, I'm a guest, a tourist—
"Have I seen the yesteryear house of Vincenti Paul
or the ancient Krakow gate?"

Oh city of centuries!—But it is spring in Lublin,
the pharmacist hums a Viennese waltz
and smoothes her blond hair in a small mirror...

קריסטלעכע אַלט־שטאָט

יאָרהונדערטער דרימלען בײַ די טעאַטאָארן,
זײ טרינקען ווײַן און זײַנען פֿול מיט סוד,
אַלכעמיע, טײַוול געמישט מיט גאָט,
און די הערצער האַלטן אין אײן גאַרן.

אין די אויגן — חכמה פֿון גענאַרן:
— דער שטערן זאָגט: טויט איז אויף דײַן טראָט,
— כ׳צאַפּ ווײַן פֿון וואַנט און שיכּור כ׳וואָר ווי לוט,
אין אַלע ווינקלען לויערן געפֿאָרן.

ווײַן אָ, לירע, פֿון סטרונעס רינט מיט דעמער,
פֿאַרשײַטקייט רײַסט זיך: נעם מיך, נעם מיך,
״אײַן מערקן אויס אַלטער צײַט פֿאַרגעסן״.

דאָן־זשואַן טראָגט זײַן ליבסטער דורך אַ פֿענצטער,
פֿיסטוילן־קנאַל, יאָגן רײַטערס און געשפֿענסטער,
ווײַן מײַן לירע, טויט איז די פּרינצעסין.

The Lublin Poems: In Lublin's Christian Old-City

Centuries slumber at the sidewalk
as if drunk with the alchemy of a mysterious
wine mixed by both the devil and God—
                    but still my heart keeps yearning:

In the eyes the cleverness of deception,
on the forehead a prophecy of death
                    flashes like a star.
I drain the vaults of wine, drunk as Lot—
                    but in every corner danger lurks.

Cry, oh lyre, your strings leak wantonness
at twilight—take me, take me
laments its ancient, forgotten tale...

and even Don Juan crashes his most beloved thru' a window
as horsemen and bystanders give chase, pistols cracking—
                    but cry oh lyre, the princess is dead.

באַך אין מינאָר

בעט מיך איבער מיט גאָט,
כ'שטיי זינדיק ביי זיין שוועל
און שעם זיך ווייטער צו גיין.

מיט אויגן פֿול געוויין
שטייט די גאַנצע וועלט,
זי ווינקט נישט מער מיט פֿאַרפֿירערישע פֿייערן,
מיט טויזנט שטעט אויף זיך און מיט שטערן
איז זי אָרעם און אַליין,
ווי אַ פּויער
אָפּגעברענט אַלע זיינע שייערן, —

און אַז מיין וואָרט איז בלינד
און ווייס נישט ווו צו גיין,
זאָל דער ניגון דערגיין
און אויסגעפֿינען אַלע אָנהייבן און סופֿן,
און אַז ס'האָט גאָט מיך געטאָן שטראָפֿן
מיט טויט וואָס ליגט אין מיר ווי אַ וואָלד
העלף מיר אין אַ מזלדיקער שעה אים געווינען,
לויטער אַזוי און אָן אַ שאָטן,
ווי אויפֿן בוים דער בלאַט,
וואָס אין זיין ביסל גרינען
איז ער אויך אין גאָט געראָטן.

בעט מיך איבער מיט גאָט,
לאָמיך ווערט זיין זיין געגנאַד,
ווי דו, ניגון, וואָס ביסט פֿון אים ארויסגעגעוואָקסן,
וווייל כאָטש אַ ווערעמל איז מיין טראָט,
איז פֿאַרפֿלאַנצט אין מיר זיין סוד
ווי אין די גאַלאַקסן.

Prayer to Bach in a Minor Key

Reconcile me with God
as I stand in sin at his threshold
ashamed to try going further.

The whole world stands here too
with tear-filled eyes, no longer able
to wink away their tricky outrages
or their thousands of cities in flames.
They are as impoverished and bereft as a peasant
who has himself burnt down all his barns.

And if my words are blind
and do not know how to proceed,
let your melody reach out and find for me
where to begin and how to end.
So when God chooses to punish me with
the death that grows within me like a fetus,
help me in a fortunate hour to gain access
to him like the littlest leaf on a tree,
which indeed in its greening is God.

Reconcile me with God;
make me worthy of his grace
just as your inspired melody can.
Though my steps inch forward as slowly
as a little worm's, your secret shall be
implanted in me as if in the galaxies.

1958

אין ניגון אײַנגעהערט

עם מוזיקאַלאַג. ישׂראל ראַבינאָװיטש

שטילער, שטילער, שטיל
שפּיל.
נאַר מיך אָפּ, נאַר מיך אָפּ,
זאָג מיר עפּעס צו,
װאַרף אַ גראָשן בלויז,
(װי ס׳פֿלעגט דער רבי װאַרפֿן
אויפֿן חומש מיר).
לאָמיך גלײבן, אַז דער מלאך
האָט מיר אים געװאָרפֿן.

איך בין אַזוי מיד פֿון חכמה אייגענער
און פֿרעמדער,
טו מיך אויס ביז זיך אַליין
פֿון אַלינקע געװענדער.
(קינדער גייען אין בלויזע העמדער
און זײנען אַלץ איינס דאָס װאָס זיי
זײנען:
פֿאַרגליבט אין אַלץ און שיין).

שפּיל, אַ שפּיל, געפֿין מיך אויס,
די מאַמע רופֿט מיר נאָך אַלץ
אין דרויסן אַרויס.
סע קומט אָן די נאַכט
און צײַט שוין צומאַכן די לאָדן,
די מאַמע האָט שוין אַלע לאָדן פֿאַרמאַכט
און איך בין געבליבן אין דרויסן,

In Melody Absorbed

—for the musicologist Israel Rabinowich

Play quietly, more quietly, still more quietly…
delude me, deceive me
promise me something
throw even just a coin—
(as the Rabbi used to drop one
on the Pentateuch after I'd recited—)
let me still believe an angel
threw it from above.

I am so weary of wisdom, mine and others—
undress me to my naked self, my very being,
denude me of all my clothing until I am
a newborn with only its undershirt
and its beautiful blind faith in everything.

Play oh play on, discover me
like my mother did who still urges me
to go outdoors but then
when night comes closes the shutters
calls me no more and I must stay forever the outsider.

Comfort me, console me
with a little lie,
the yesterday's day,
that brings me heaven-preserve-us
much ado about nothing
until I just up and die
for truth is so harsh, so difficult
and no one promises anything.

און סע רופֿט מיר קיינער נישט מער.
טרייסט מיר, אַ טרייסט מיר
מיט אַ ביסעלע ליגן:
ברענג מיר דעם נישט דאָ געדאַכט,
נעכטיקע טעג,
אויפֿן הימל אַ יאַריד.

אָט אָ נעם איך און שטאַרב
און דער אמת איז האַרב,
אַזוי שווער און האַרב,
און קיינער זאָגט גאָרנישט צו

זע, איך האַלט בײַם קבֿר שוין,
און ראָזשינקעס מיט מאַנדלען
האָט אַ האַנט פֿון מײַן וויגל צוגערויבט
און קערט זיי מיר נישט אום.

לאָמיך נישט ערגער זײַן ווי די גאַנצע וועלט,
וועמען דו האַלטסט אין איין געבן צו פֿארשטיין
ווי עלנט זי איז;
ווײַנסט פֿאַר איר,
זוכסט אַרום איר פֿאַרפֿאַלן קינד,

ברעקלסטו פֿאַר ווייטיק שורות הזהר
אין די גאַסן
און שטעלסט זיי אויס איינזאַם
אין מיטן פֿעלד,
שטיבעלעך בײַם ים וואַסער
מיט שקיעה אין די פֿענצטער,
מאַכסטו דעמערן פֿון טעג
און פֿולע טיבן בענקשאַפֿט.

Look, I stand now nearly at my grave
and the almonds and raisins that the lullaby
promised to me a hand has stolen from my cradle
never to be returned.

Oh God let me not fare any worse than the whole world
while you keep lamenting how forlorn it all is
and for which you cry as if seeking a lost child.

God, because of your pain you break
apart rows of houses huddled in streets
and instead placed them in solitude
in the midst of fields—
small houses beside water
with sunset in the windows;
transform day into twilight
and fill rivers with longing.

Oh, promise me at least something—
that the tree leaves fluttering away in
autumn, like handkerchiefs at leave-taking,
those leaves
will return
though they never come back the same.

אָ זאָג מיר עפּעס צו,
ווי ביימער פֿאָכען אין האַרבסט מיט
די בלעטער
ווי מיט טיכלעך ביים געזעגענען:
— מיר קומען צוריק,
כאָטש זיי קומען קיין מאָל די זעלבע
נישט צוריק.

אַזוי זעט אויס דאָס געזאַנג פֿון בלומען: וויסער וויַין,
אַזוי בליבסטו, ליד מיַינס, ווען כ׳וועל שוין מער נישט זיַין.

און ווי יענער טרויער וואָס פֿאַרגייט זיך שטיל אין דופֿט,
און ס׳הויכט אַ מאַנטל אויס אים אין דער לופֿט.

און סע וויינט די שיידונג אויפֿן טראָטואַר,
וואָלקנס זיַינען שוואַרצער קרעפּ פֿון צער,

אַ ביַנטל יאָרן, ווי מטבעות אויסגעשיט,
פֿאַלן צו פֿאַרשוויינדנדיקע טריט.

פֿון אַלע שויבן דרינגט אַצינד די קלאָג,
ווי דער אומעט וואָס פֿאַרשפּרייט אַ ליכט בײַ טאָג,

אַזוי זעט אויס דאָס געזאַנג פֿון בלומען: וויסער וויַין
אַזוי בליבסטו ליד מיַינס, ווען כ׳וועל שוין מער נישט זיַין.

Perfume

This is how the song of flowers seems: white wine
evaporating but its bouquet lingering like songs of mine.

This grief that appears to dissipate quickly into thin air
still clings to my clothes and my hair.

Parting cries that follow my path without relief
from the black crepe cloud of grief.

A bundle of years scattered like coins, wept over,
disappearing like footsteps.

The sadness that takes away
from every windowpane the lightness of day.

This is how the song of flowers seems: white wine
evaporating, yet its bouquet lingering like songs of mine.

לאָמיר פֿאַרהאַלטן דעם זומער

לאָמיר פֿאַרהאַלטן דעם זומער,
לאָמיר אים פֿאַרהאַלטן,
לאָמיר דעם גרינעם גערויש זײַנעם באַהאַלטן,
לאָמיר אים אָנבינדן בײַם שטאַרקן בוים.
הינטערן בוים איז דאָ אַ שטיער
און טירן שטײַען אָפֿן.

די רויטע אויפֿגעגנג לאָזן איבער צווײַטן בלאַסע,
און פֿון די פֿאַרנאַכטן בלײַבן העלע פֿאַסן,
לאָמיר זיך פֿאַרגאָרטלען מיט זיי,
לאָמיר זיי פֿאַרבינדן
צו די שטאַרקע פֿלאַנצן, וואָס ציִען זיך פֿון וואַסער,
לאָמיר פֿאַרבאַהאַלטן דעם זומער,
לאָמיר אים פֿאַרנאַרן,
אין די טיפֿע טאָלן — וועלטס ליבעוווּנדן,
לאָמיר אים נישט לאָזן שײדן.

Let's Detain the Summer

Let's detain the summer;
let's hold fast to him;
let's hide his green rustling;
let's tie him to a strong tree.
Behind the tree there's a barn
and the doors stand open.

The red sunrises trail pale tufts of hair;
and the sunset's light-streaks linger;
let's put them on like a sash;
let's tie them
to the strongest plants that extend themselves from the water;
let's hide the summer; let's entice him
into the deep valleys—the world's love wounds.
Let's not allow him to part.

די פֿידל

כ׳זאָג דיר: מען דאַרף האָבן כּוח,
געדולד דאַרף מען האָבן בשעת
עס גיט אַ צעקריג זיך די פֿידל,
אין מיטן דער שפּיל מיטן באַס.

וואָס איז געשען? נו זאָג זשע,
די יונגפֿרוי, די פֿידל, זי בענקט,
זי האָט אַ פֿאַרגעסענע ליבע
פלוצעם אין שפּילן געדענקט.

אין וועמען פֿאַרליבט זיך אַ פֿידל?
אַוודאי אין נעכטיקע טעג,
דער באַס — איר מאַן אויף דער עלטער,
אָט וואַרפֿט ער זיך גלײַך אין געשלעג,

און ברומט ווי אַ בער אויס זײַן בו בו,
אַזאַ מין איינטאָניק געברום,
אַזוי ווי די שעהען וואָס קריכן
פּוסט אַרום זייגער אַרום.

און זי, די פֿידל, זי פֿרוווט זיך
אים נעמען מיט גוטינקע רייד:
— כ׳בין דאָך ניט מער ווי אַ פֿידל,
וואָס גלײַכסטו מיך צו צום טרומפּייט?

יענער געוווינט איז צום טומל,
זײַן סוד איז אַ סוד פֿאַר גאַנץ בראָד,
נאָר ער מאַכט אַרום אַזאַ ליאַרעם
ווי ער וואָלט עס געפֿונען אַ גאָט.

The Violin

I tell you: You need strength,
patience is still needed
when the violin starts a quarrel
with the bass in the midst of a familiar duet.

What happens then: Do tell,
the supposedly innocent violin keeps on lamenting
the all-but-forgotten love of her youthful days
about which she incessantly weeps as she plays.

And who it was: The violin just repeats and repeats,
but of course the love song is now just rote memory
and the bass, her partner in this condescending duo,
immediately answers back with fierce notes.

And then: The bass begins to growl and grovel
like a bear—boo—boo—boo,
mindlessly beeping around the clock.

And so: The violin tries seduction
with some pianissimo wailing—
saying I am only a fragile, finely tuned violin,
don't treat me like a trumpet strumpet!

Ah but: The bear is used to being overbearing,
it's not a secret anymore,
so he creates a stormy crescendo
as though he's just discovered God.

Only then: The wailing begins anew—
how she used to hide her scherzos,
her tiniest joys from her tears, but never
could choke back more than a few.

און איך בין געוווינט צו באַהאַלטן
אַפֿילו מײַן פיצעלע גליק,
און אין די אייגענע טרערן
ווער איך נישט איין מאָל דערשטיקט.

נאָר וואָס פֿאַרשטייט זיך אַ באַס דען,
ער הויבט אויף אַ גראָשן פֿון מיסט,
און צו די הימלען דער פֿידל
באַלד וועט זיך גיבן אַ ריס.

But I tell you: The bass, who isn't listening any more
becomes increasingly violent, descending
upon the violin with a cacophony that
drowns her in an onslaught of filthy accusations.

דזשאַז

ייִנגעלע, דאָס פֿעטערל איז צעדרייט:
ר׳האָט אָנגעטאָן די זון ווי אַ מיצל אויפֿן קאָפּ,
די אַרבל אַרויף, דעם קאָלנער אַראָפּ,
און די שטערנס אין מאַנטל אײַנגענייט.

ער שפּילט אויפֿן וועלדל ווי אויף אַ קאַם,
און ס׳איז דאָס וואָלקנדל זײַן ביבעלע־פּאַפּיר,
וויי איז מיר, ס׳איז זײַן ציר
די גראָבע ריײד פֿון שיכורן קאַם.

ייִנגעלע, אַנטלויף, אַנטלויף,
פֿעטערל האָט אַלע טויערן פֿאַרמאַכט,
און פֿרי געמאַכט נאַכט, כאָטש ס׳איז ווײַט צו נאַכט,
און ליגט אין ווינקל מיד באַזויפֿט.

156

Jazz

Little boy, your uncle is crazy, hatless,
but he wears the sun like a hat on his head,
his sleeves are rolled up, his collar rolled down.
and stars are sewn to his coat.

He plays on the wood as if it were a comb,
and a small cloud is his little notebook,
woe is me, it's his ornament for the
the coarse words of a drunken boor.

Little boy, run away, run away
uncle has closed all the city gates
and made night come early, though it's not time,
but he lies in a corner tired and drunk.

צו איינער

און צו דיר נייגן זיך אַזוי פּשוט מײַנע מעת־לעתן,
אַלע מײַנע שיינע ניגונים לאָז איך איבער,
כ'ווייס אַז דיר איז ליבער
אַ נאַרישע טאַנגאָ, וואָס כ'האָב לאַנג שוין פֿאַרגעסן.

אויף אַלע מײַנע בריוו שרײַב איך איבער די אַדרעסן,
ים אַריבער, לאַנד אַריבער, לעבן אַריבער,
צום שטיבעלע דעמער, צום נישט־דאָ׳ִקן פֿיבער,
צו אַ ווײַטן שטערן, צו דײַן וועזן.

158

To Someone

And it is simply to you every hour
of day and night that I bow down,
and to you I bequeath my pretty melodies,
though I know you prefer that silly tango
I have long forgotten.

I rewrite your addresses on each letter
I send you over the oceans, over the lands,
my whole life over—letters from me to that
small bit of twilight, that absent fervor.

וויוואַלדי

אויף אַלע דײַנע פֿאַרפֿלאַנטערטע וועגעלעך
גיי איך געהאָרכזאַם דיר נאָך.

אָוונטשײַן וועט די שכינה זײַן,
ביז שױבן וועלן נעמען וווּנדער דערזען.

די גאַנצע וועלט ווערט עק גאַס צום פֿעלד אַרויס,
דעם שיינעם טרויער צו באַגעגענען.

דורות שטייען קעפּ אויף קעפּ,
און איך האַלט נאָך בײַם אומעט פֿון טרעפּ.

וואָס זײַנען יאָרן? ווי זײַנען מײַנע יאָרן?
אין מיר דער טרויער פֿון ליידיקע קאָרידאָרן.

עמעץ גייט אַדורך, עמעץ שליסט אויף אַ טיר
און לאָזט דעם קלאַנג פֿון שלאָס איבער מיר.

מײַן כּלה לערנט זיך אַ קנויילעכל אויפֿצובינדן,
די מאַמע זאָל צום שידוך מסכּים זײַן.

Vivaldi

I follow your entangled little ways
through the maze in my ears,

until twilight becomes the Divine Presence
and, in my mind, the windows reflect miracles.

The whole world becomes a street vanishing into fields;
it yields to an exquisite grief.

Generations stand crowded head to head,
but I still have the sadness of stairs fled.

What are years? Where are my years?
Within me are only the tears of empty corridors.

Someone passes by, someone unlocks a door,
and it leaves the click hovering forever...

My bride is learning to untangle a ball of wool
so my mother will agree to the match in full.

אין שטילן, קילן הויז פֿון דעם סאָנעט
איך רײַס, ווי אַ גזלן זיך אַרײַן בײַ נאַכט,
דאָס גאַנצע הויזגעזינד איז געוואָרן וואַך,
דעם באַלעבאָס איך שלעפּ אַרויס פֿון בעט.

— ״אַבי קיל יו״ — קאַלטער, אַלטער שד,
מיליאָנער פֿון שטילן טראַכט און דאַכט,
דאָ ליגט אַ וועלט ווי אַ שיף וואָס קראַכט
און דו ביסט אַלץ וויִכער גלעט, געבעט.

דאָס שטילע, קילע הויז פֿון דעם סאָנעט
איך צענעם אַזוי־אַ ברעט נאָך ברעט
און גזל רו וואָס מײַן האַרץ עס פֿעלט.

מ׳וועט מיך יאָגן לויט די צייכנס שרעק
און אומרו צעשאָטן אויפֿן וועג,
לויפֿנדיק אין דעם עק פֿון וועלט.

162

To the Sonnet

In the quiet, cool house of the sonnet
I enter forcefully, like a robber at night.
The whole household awakens in fright,
I pull the owner out of bed.

—"I kill you"—cold, old ghost,
millions of quiet thoughts and fantasies
lie here like a crashed ship,
all the more you are a soft caress, a plea.

The quiet, cool house of the sonnet
I take apart board by board, like this,
and steal the peace of which my heart has a dearth.

They will pursue me by the signs of fear
and unrest scattered on the road,
running at the edge of the earth.

Notes to Section III

"A Mite That Dies": Written in 1932 when Emiot was twenty-three. He actually learned that his father died in poverty one year after leaving for New York City to become a doctor when Emiot was ten. He left many books, both religious and secular, behind. The poem, written well before Emiot's return to Lublin in 1957 from a Gulag, was chosen by him to begin this cycle of poems.

"Old Lublin": Jacob Glatstein, was born in Lublin, emigrated to New York City, and was a distinguished and much published Yiddish poet. Whether Emiot had visited Lublin prior to 1958 or not, he surely knew it to be a place of real consequence for Jews and in Glatstein's oeuvre.

"Untitled #2" ("Like an eviscerated..."): Yatecoveh Street, a street in the former Jewish district close to the Maharoshe Synagogue. It does not exist today.

The Ne'ilah, last prayer said at Yom Kippur Service on the very solemn Day of Atonement.

Maharoshe Synagogue, named after Shloime Luria 1510- 1573, who wrote commentaries on religious tracts and included important historical information re: rabbis of Germany of that period. Rabbi of Lublin.

"Untitled #3" ("Covered wagons rumble..."): Moshe Montalto, a Sephardic physician who settled in Poland in the seventeenth century and built a synagogue in Lublin. He transformed the prayer liturgy, (the Nusach), into a more Kabbalistic document, using the Sephardic languages. To understand Emiot's evoking an image of Dr. Montalto, one has to realize that he too came from an Chasidic family tradition and was reaching back toward that philosophic position which was also prevalent although less institutionalized in Lublin at that time. In Chasidic belief joyous singing and dance provided a more direct connection to God than the synagogues and rabbis.

"Untitled #5" ("Where is the sun…"): Kol Nidre, prayer for the dead.

"The International," the name of the Communist International Anthem

"Blood Accusation," the ancient but still espoused false belief that Jews engage in ritual murder to obtain the blood of Christian children to use in religious activities such as Passover.

"Untitled #6" ("Sad wedding music…"): Tishev -B'Ov, the day of lamentation for the destruction of the Temples, etc.

"In Maharoshe Synagogue": Maharoshe Synagogue: By a special privilege granted to the Jews of Lublin by King Zygmut August, in 1567, Jews were allowed to build a brick synagogue to honor Rabbi Shlomo Luria who died in 1537. It became the main synagogue. It was burnt in 1655 along with the Jewish town, then rebuilt; it collapsed in 1854 but was again rebuilt in 1864 in classic style and dominated its surroundings. A huge bimah supported the dome of a spacious square praying chamber. It was destroyed during WW2.

Maharoshe, or Maharshal, was a famous Chasidic leader actually named Yechiel Luria. He taught that "The Divine Presence does not rest on a man plunged in gloom, but only in the midst of joy."

Rama: This master taught that alarm may be sounded on account of any calamity that comes upon a community except excessive rain: "We should not pray for the cessation of superabundant blessing, for it is said, 'I will surely open for you the windows of heaven and pour out a blessing for you that there shall be more than enough.' However, in the Diaspora Rama bar R. Judah said 'the alarm may be sounded on account of such superabundance… so that their houses may not become their graves.'"

(Note: In Lublin, the tension between the more institutionalized religious philosophy and practices, and that of the more ecstatic Chasidic tradition, was much in evidence.)

"Untitled #8" ("The keeper of this cemetery lives..."): The Yabbok Book: Prayers and customs for the sick and dying and rules of mourning, published in Modena in 1626 and in Amsterdam, 1725.

"Old Jewish Cemetery" ("Oh, generations..."): Old Jewish Cemetery, established 1490. Grodzisko Hill was a fortified town until the thirteenth century. Jews were allowed one third for a cemetery officially in 1555, then all of it in the seventeenth century. Surrounded by a stone wall at that time, earth mounds one meter thick were eventually added to the burial area, which allowed it to function until 1829, when an additional cemetery was built elsewhere. Because of Grodzisko Hill's strategic location it was often devastated in military campaigns. However, most of its tombstones were used by the Nazis in the construction of the primarily wooden Majdanek Concentration Camp on the outskirts of Lublin. Nevertheless, a few very historically important tombstones remain.

Vincenti Paul was a well-known poet born in Lublin in 1872. His house is now a museum. He was very interested in geography and he was the father of tourism in the Lublin region. It is now an historic area of architectural diversity.

"In Lublin's Christian Old-City": Lot, in Genesis (and the Koran) is the nephew of Abraham. At God's command this lone good man leaves Sodom with his wife and daughters. His wife looks back and turns into a pillar of salt. His daughters seduce him after he is drugged with wine, ostensibly to perpetuate their lineage. The eldest daughter's son is Moab (Moabites). The younger's son is Beninmi (Ammonites).

Don Juan, the ultimate seducer of allegedly 1,000 women, is found in Spanish legend, the poetry of Byron, and Mozart's opera Don Giovanni, etc. A symbol of false passion and carnality. He is killed at the grave of the princess by her father.

"In Melody Absorbed": Traditional: A coin or a drip of honey was dropped on the successfully read Pentateuch or hand of the child performing the reading, from behind and / or above, allegedly by an angel but really by the Rabbi. This was a reward for young children who were just learning to read.

(A kind of Jewish tooth fairy!) A teacher and a rabbi were often differentiated, but the words used were similar.

"A yesterday's day": An idiom for an impossibility or improbability/a trivia, of no consequence.

Raisins and Almonds: Very well known and emotional lullaby, promising, "If you go to sleep you shall have raisins and almonds." Was especially poignant because of poverty.

"Vivaldi": "ball of wool": Traditionally, as a test of character, a prospective daughter-in-law was given a tangled ball of yarn to unravel and rewind.

Section IV

1966–1978

United States

From Before You Extinguish Me, For the Sake of Ten, Siberia *(Translation)*, *and* Strays

IN 1966 EMIOT PUBLISHED the poetry book, *Before You Extinguish Me*, in Rochester, New York, in Yiddish. It again contained the Siberia cycle, which was ultimately published for the first time in my English translation, with an introductory essay, by State Street Press, in 1991. However, *Before You Extinguish Me*, printed in New York, again contained recycled poems from his prior years. At the same time, it also contained a significant number of new and contemporary poems that pertained to his life in the United States. It should also be noted that all his Yiddish books published after 1958 were done so with subsidy by the Jewish Community Center or specific individuals. *For the Sake of Ten*, published in 1969, contains much prose as well. The poems I have designated as "strays" I discovered in five water-logged boxes in the basement of the Jewish Community Center in Rochester after his death. Many were unpublished, and often barely legible or provisional drafts handwritten on scrap paper, stray envelopes, memo sheets, and what not. Clearly Emiot was trying to create a new book manuscript, again patching, rescuing, and writing anew—just a few years before dying of a brain tumor in 1978.

Before You Extinguish Me, over and above the Siberia cycle, contains some very accomplished poetry. The title poem develops one of Emiot's most striking and eloquent themes about the relationship between nature and man, life and death, "the world's strange cat and mouse game." "The End of a Story" is set on the shores of Lake Ontario, and asks that he be allowed to live again in his childhood memory of little boats ...on a cradle of waves." "Hour of Sadness" uses a planetary metaphor to highlight his loneliness, saying, "I have given myself a divorce many times...." There are also musings on growing older. In the poem "Los Angeles," written on a train trip west, he adopts an image from Goethe to express the idea of recovery and renewal and couches it in the idea of climate change. Likewise the poem "Arizona Desert" looks forward to his grandchild's generation, but backwards to the biblical saga of the Jews in the desert. "Nightfall," a fantasy poem, envisions power and reward that he wishes he had but knows he does not. But reality impinges with the poem "Friends Are Dying Out," which also mentions "Vivaldi's soft song." Again, music becomes his poetic vehicle in the untitled poem beginning "To hold on to Mozart's movement/and thus remain suspended...." The often quoted poem, "As Long As We Are Not Alone," speaks directly about rejoicing at human contact: "Perhaps the stone also hears?" But again, that sentiment is countered in the poem called "Stores" (included in Section II), which describes the emptiness of streets at night. Then comes the forlorn gesture of displacement in "Our Mothers Will Not Be at Our Deaths." Since the book begins with the rather philosophical if impassioned title poem, it is fitting that the personal lament about his mother should be followed by a poem called "Thus," which directly addresses growing old: "you meet yourself as quite another/...wandering/... to a goal that is no goal."

The *Siberia* poems are often Petrarchan sonnets in the original. They pivot between the past and the present as a way of coping with the Gulag, but gradually the harsh current reality of being there takes precedence as well as conveying vivid descriptions of people and surroundings. Pulled into this cycle is the poem "The Everlasting," which was originally published in 1936:

> With or without me
> days will pass to their harsh death
>
> I will be a flower then, or perhaps something else.
>
> It's no big deal to die.

Noteworthy poems in this cycle include ones about snow, anticipation of life after the Gulag, inmate thieves and friends, weather, roll calls, moments of nostalgia, his elderly grandmother, and references to early religious lore. Biblical quotes and dedications abound, even though opportunity to write these poems out was almost non-existent under Gulag conditions. As with the Lublin series of sonnets and related poems, the Siberian ones have much formal structure and successfully sustain both a mood and a body of information, and were certainly envisioned as a sequence by Emiot. To illustrate the mood of this Siberia group of poems, and contrast them to the even darker Lublin series, a few of the specifically Gulag related poems are reprinted in this book. They are: "Dreamsongs," the first of the sonnets, "How many days and ways have passed—/as much distance from me to me/as from Poland to Siberia?" which begins with recall of the past and ends with the reality of the Gulag. There is the poem about "Melave Malke" nights and tales of the Bal Shem

Tov, the legendary Chasidic wonder worker, "the moon slips away; it has never been so distant, so shy of my eye." Several poems are laced with dark, sardonic humor. "Oginski's Polonaise" begins with the fiercely harsh weather conditions at the Gulag by talking of the sustaining music of Oginski, a famous Polish composer. "Prayer of a Man in Snow," which is in free verse and a very simple and repetitious form, quotes from the Book of Daniel, and conveys the horror and potential doom of a relentlessly snowy vista on end, and couples it with references to traditional Jewish prayers that unfold during a typical, prayer-filled orthodox day. "Dreamed-Up Still Life" is another very simple, one could say stark, poem which indulges in anticipation of "A lovely, clear, glass of tea...," etc.

For the Sake of Ten contains one especially subtle poem called "To a Woman Violinist." Using a well-known and variously translated image from the Song of Songs, Emiot develops a commentary on how the violin, like an ornamental shield, adorns the violinist's neck when playing the music of Saint-Saen. He follows this with his connection to her and the music. Like so many of his poems about music and his emotions, it is very complex, because he is able to extend the poem to both the personal and the worldly realm.

The so-called "stray" poems, including those shifted over from earlier books, are mainly in free verse, and unmistakably contemporary in their directness of diction and form. They are sometimes experimental, frequently urban in setting, and unremittingly alienated, dislocated and lovelorn. Sometimes they try to make the best of it all. Other times they are bitter or bereft. Musical imagery is often still present. As if unwittingly to register the shock of coming to the United States, this tentative collection begins with a poem called "The Sickly Little Boy," a response to the Biafran conflict that reminded him of the Holocaust. It was printed in a Yiddish newspaper in 1975. "I Follow Myself Alone" harkens back to his experiments with triolets, though it is not one, yet it has something of the pastoral sense of his use of that form. Likewise, "Lead Me" reaches back to the purer Assyrian era font to make the point that the world has both good and evil people in it. Yet in "Stillness" he argues, with himself, that "You still don't need very much to be happy." In the "Untitled" poem beginning "Many stairs lead down," he makes strong reference to the poem "Credo," by the Hebrew poet Saul Tchernikovsky—a well known poem of affirmation. Again, "Untitled" says, "Ropes bind me to this harbor...," i.e. to memories of two lovers. In the untitled "To the quiet holiday of your radiant face," Emiot writes of love by referring to the Adam and Eve story in which Adam is made of clay by the Golem. There is the untitled poem, "There is still a place to hide." Then, shifting unmistakably to a city setting, he speaks of aloneness in the midst of tall buildings entrapped in inner turmoil. Another untitled poem laments that "She is also still not the one." "He Doesn't Love Her" attempts to explain that. While "Song" says that he is as empty as a vacated house, and spring no longer conceivable. The poem "Empty" says, "I beg you not to expect much of me." An untitled poem speaks of the edge of the city where he will dance with his healthy leg and cry with his sick one. This poem is followed by the pop culture notion of the girl in the magazine's advertisement, which Emiot then links with "why God at the beauty/of the rainbow vowed/there would never be a flood again." "Hospital Reflections," 1975, published in a Yiddish journal called *The Future,* expresses a range of feelings about his nurse, her kindnesses, the specter of death, and human rapport. In the untitled poem beginning, "Mature now in years and musical tastes," he speaks of both loss and happiness. The poem "On Both of Us Listening to Bach" again uses an extended musical metaphor to suggest that it is important to become open to what can happen in a life or relationship, which can linger in memory and meaning despite the passage of time, distance and irrevocable circumstances. Another stray, originally in an earlier book, is "Don't Leave Me Alone," in which "Night cuts itself/into four black mirrors/...don't leave me alone." raditionally mirrors were shrouded in a household at the time of a death. This poem can be considered a companion piece in spirit to the oft-quoted "As Long As We Are Not Alone."

It is also clear, and important, that Emiot meant to include, from earlier collections, "As Long As We Are Not Alone," "Tango," "Perfume," "Hour of Sadness," "Hour of All Hours," "Just Like This," and perhaps others he had yet to write or revise. The ordering of these stray poems is actually somewhat arbitrary, since Emiot had not finalized the collection.

My intent in organizing the contents of this book into four roughly chronological sections corresponding to geographical locations was to afford the reader some sense of Emiot's life and times. Who knows what more Emiot might have written if he had not been forced by circumstances to spend so much of his life in transit, and his last years in the rescue and reconstruction of his life's literary creations, or in the frustrating effort to learn yet another language, find truly literary translators, discover new friends, and revive a modicum of health and well-being. Would he have been able to connect in his writing more to the current society and events in which he found himself? Would his work have taken new and startling paths in form as well? Would he have added to his considerable production of short and long fiction, or his essays? Suffice to say there was much to admire about his talent, his persistence in writing honestly about his inner self, as well as his drastically changing surroundings and circumstances, and his insistence on perceiving himself as a worthy, hard working writer unto the end of his life. Coincidentally, Emiot participated in the reinvigoration of the Yiddish language, its literature, and its archives.

איידער דו לעשסט מיך אויס

איידער דו לעשסט מיך אויס —
נעם דאָס גרין פֿון די ביימער אַרויס,
לאָז דאָס גרין זיבן מאָל גרינער ווערן ווי ס׳איז,
און יעדער שטראַל זאָל דערגיין מיר ווי אַ שפּיז.
און זיבן מאָל העכער זאָל ווערן יעדן פֿויגלס טרעל,
און דער הימל זאָל אַראָפּלאָזן זיך צו מײַן קלײַנער שוועל.

לעש מיך אויס, נאָר לעש נישט אויס, מײַן גאָט,
דעם טאָג איידער ער אַנטפּלעקט זײַן סוד,
און ביז מײַן לעצטער רגע נישט שטיל אין מיר דעם דאָרשט,
צו אַלץ וואָס איך באַוווּנדער, צו אַלעס וואָס איך פֿאָרש,
פֿריִער דאָס גערויש, דערנאָך דאָס ווערן שטיל
דאָס מאָדנע, אין דער וועלט, קאַץ־און־מויז־געשפּיל.

176

Before You Extinguish Me

Before you extinguish me—
take out the green from the trees.
Let the green become seven times greener,
and every ray reach me like a spear.
Let each bird's trill become seven times higher
and the sky lower itself to my little threshold.

Extinguish me, my God, but don't extinguish the day
before its secrets are revealed.
Until my last moments do not quench my thirst
for all I hold in wonder, all I seek.
First the rustling, then the resting—
the world's strange cat and mouse game.

מיר זיינען שוין צו ביסלעך זקנים

מיר זיינען שוין צו ביסלעך זקנים,
קלאַפּן צו מיט אַ פֿינגער אויף אַ שיינעם ניגון,
וואָס מיר האָבן שוין אַ מאָל טויזנט געהערט,
מיר רעדן אַלץ וועגן וועטער:
"היינט וועט די זון שיינען"
מיר קערן זיך אום צו היינען,
צו געטען.
זאָגן כסדר:
— מסתמא איז אַזוי באַשערט,
קלאָגן זיך צו ביסלעך אויף דער ראיה,
זוכן עפּעס צו שוועענקען,
און סטאַרען זיך עס זאָל כאָטש אַ תּנועה
בלייבן פֿון זיך
אַן אייניקל צו שענקען,
צום געדענקען.

Bit by Bit We've Already Become Old

Bit by bit we've already become old.
Our fingers tap a catchy tune
we've already heard a thousand times.
We keep talking about the weather:
"Today the sun will shine."
We return to Heine,
to Goethe,
incessantly saying:
"Probably it is so ordained"—
complaining a bit about our sight,
looking for something with which to gargle,
and trying to retain at least
one of our remaining gestures
to gift a grandchild with as a remembrance.

סוף מעשה

שטראָף מיך מיט אַלץ
נאָר לאָז מיך זײַן קינד,
ס׳איז גענוג אַ צעוויג
אין מיטן אָנטאַריאָ־ים,
און אַלע שיפֿעלעך קומען צוריק
וואָס כ׳האָב אַ מאָל אין קינדהייט
געשיקט זיי מיטן וואַסער,

כ׳האַלט ביי סוף מעשה
נאָר די מעשה הייבט זיך ערשט אָן,
כ׳וויין נאָך אַלץ אויף מײַן שׂימחת־תּורה־פֿאָן
פּונקט ווי אויף מײַן האַרץ צעגערויבטס
און כ׳וואַרט נאָך אַלץ אָפּ דער מאַמען דורכן שויב
כאָטש מײַן אייניקל וואַקסט מיר ביי די קני.

180

The End of the Story

Punish me with everything
but let me be childlike;
it's enough that a cradle of waves
in the middle of Lake Ontario
rocks back from every direction
all the little boats I once had in childhood
which I sent with the water;

I am on the verge of the end of the story,
only now the story has just begun:
Still I'm crying over my Simkhes-Toyre flag
exactly as I cry over my stolen heart,
and still I'm waiting for my mother at the window pane
though my grandchild grows at my knee.

שעה פֿון אומעט

שעה פֿון אומעט,
אַלע שעהען רעגענען
און אַלץ איז נאָענט
און אַלץ איז פֿול מיט געזעגענען,
איך לעב נאָך אַלץ,
כאָטש כ׳האָב וויפֿל מאָל געגעבן
זיך אַליין אַ גט,
נאָר איך דריי זיך נאָך אַלץ
ווי אַ וויטער פּלאַנעט
אַרום דיר,
פֿון עפּעס אַן אומבאַקאַנטן געזעץ
געצוווּנגען.
מיט אַזוי פֿיל רינגען
נעמסטו מיך אַרום,
נאָר איך בין שטום,
אַזוי שוויַיגן
אַלע ביימער און אַלע צוויַיגן
ביז אַרויף צו די פּלאַנעטן.

Hour of Sadness

Hour of sadness
rain all the time
everything close
and full of goodbyes;
I am still living,
even though I have given myself
a divorce many times,
yet like a distant planet
I still spin myself around you,
driven
by some unknown law;
with so many things,
like Saturn's rings you encircle me,
but I am mute;
thus are silent
all the trees and all the branches
rising to the planets.

לאָס אַנגעלעס

אומרויִק און זוכנדיק און אויף ס'נײַ געליטן,
און טראָג דאָס ביסל בענקשאַפֿט פֿאַר אַיעדער שוועל,
ווי געפֿעלסטו זיך אינעם נײַעם געמעל? —
פֿאַלמעס טוען אָן דיר נײַע, גרינע היטן.

האָסט דעם טויט נישט איין מאָל אויסגעמיטן,
ערשט שווימט ער אויף מיט יעדער קליינער וועל,
כאָטש נעם גראַם העל מיט זעל,
און ציטרינען־בליטן מיט סיבירער שליטן.

ס'איז נישט דאָס לעצטע ווערק און נישט דײַן לעצטער האָפֿן,
נאָר ווי אַמאָל בײַם דריטן טאָג באַשאַפֿן
זאָג, ווי דער באַשאַפֿער, כי טובֿ, ס'איז גוט!
עס פֿעלט עפּעס און ס'וועט אַ סך נאָך פֿעלן,
נאָר אַלע פֿאַרבן שטאַרבן אָפּ אין העל
פֿון אַלע לאַנגע וועגן אויסגערוט.

184

Los Angeles

Restless, searching and suffering anew—
I carry a bit of longing for every doorstep.
How do you view yourself in that fresh landscape
where palm trees dress you in new green hats?

> More than once you've out-distanced death;
> but now he swims to the surface with each small swell,
> as if one would rhyme bright with soul's night
> and Iberian lemon blossoms with Siberian sleds.

It is not your last labor, nor your final haven;
but say, as did the Creator on the third day—
It is good. It's good!
Something is lacking, and much will always be,
but then, you see all colors die out in brightness,
even as they recover from their long journeys.

מידבר אַריזאָנאַ

גאָט העלף, באָבעשי, אין מידבר אַריזאָנאַ,
איך הער נאָך אַלץ דעם טײַטש־חומש נאָך גאַנצע דרײַסיק יאָר;
אַלץ איז אַזױ פּשוט, דאָך בלײַבט נאָך אַלץ נישט קלאָר
די פֿערציק יאָר אין מידבר, די אמתע כּװנה.

בײַ װעמען זאָל איך פֿרעגן, בײַ װעמען זאָל איך מאָנען
פֿאַר טױט פֿון דור־המידבר בײַם צוגעזאָגטן לאַנד;
פֿון מיר איז אױך דאָס גליק צו דערלאַנגען מיט דער האַנט,
נאָר די האַנט װערט מיר קורץ אין מידבר אַריזאָנאַ.

אפֿשר װעט מײַן אײניקל דערלעבן צו דעם אמת,
איך בין בלינד, אַ רמז פֿון אַ רמז.
זאָג, באָבע, נאָך אַ מאָל, צאינה וראינה, װי אַמאָל.

איז װאָס אַז נישטאָ אַפֿילו קײן רמז פֿון דײַן קבֿר,
איך קלײַב אױף דיר אַן אבֿר צו אַן אבֿר,
פֿון הר־סיני נעמט דאָס ייִנגעלע דעם אַלטן תּורה־עול.

(באַן: סאַנטאַ פֿע, על קאַפּיטאַן, ל. אַ.־שיקאַגע)

Arizona Desert

Written on the El Capitan train from Chicago to Los Angeles

God help me, darling Grandmother, in the midst of the Arizona desert
after thirty years I still hear the Yiddish translation of the books of Moses.
Everything is so simple, yet it still remains unclear
what the true intent was of the forty years in the desert.

Whom shall I ask, of whom should I demand answers
about the death of the desert generation at the edge of the promised land?
I too have had the "good luck" to reach out with my arms
only to find them foreshortened in the desert.

Hopefully my grandchild will live to see the truth,
for I am so blind all I see is an illusion of an illusion.
Grandmother, say your women's prayers once again as of old!

So what if there isn't even a hint of your grave.
I gather and assemble you limb by limb, as on Mt. Sinai—
this little boy who still takes upon himself the old yoke of Torah.

פֿריִנד שטאַרבן אויס

פֿריִנד שטאַרבן אויס, איך בלײַב אַלײן,
ווי אַ רעװאָלװער צום האַרצן — איר בליק,
אין איר אויג דאָס ביסל גרינע גליק
און דאָס זײַד פֿון איר חן.

ס׳איז צו שטיל פֿאַרן װײסן קומער,
(פֿאַרן ליד פֿאַסן נישט קיין געװאַלדן),
און איך לויש אַלץ דעם שטילן װיװאַלדין
ווי מ׳הערט אַ ניגון פֿון צװײטן צימער,

ווי דורכזיכטיקער טיול אויף איר לײַב
דער שנײיִקער צײַט־פֿאַרטרײַב,
וויפֿל איז דער שיעור צו לוישן און לוישן?

דער ניגון שעפּטשעט: כּי טובֿ, כּי טובֿ,
און באַשאַפֿט אַ װעלט — אַ בלאָען עוף
אין טויטס װיסטן מושבֿ.

188

Friends Are Dying Out

Friends are dying out; I remain alone;
like a revolver to the heart—her glance,
that little bit of green joy, that dance in her eye
and her silken charm.

It's too quiet for the white guest sorrow.
I'm still humming Vivaldi's soft song;
like a melody heard from the next room
it doesn't suit such a violent wrong.

The snow-chilling exile of time
lay on her flesh like transparent tulle.
How much longer can one hum on and on?

The melody murmurs: It's good it's good
and creates a world—a blue bird
in death's desolate dwelling.

נאַכט צו

עס וועט בלײַבן שטײן די נאַכט אויף מײַן באַפֿעל
און מײַן גאַס וועט זיך נישט צײַען ווי אַלע מאָל;
די פֿאַר בײַמער וואָס האָבן וואָס צו זאָגן וועלן אַלע זאָגן
בײַ מײַן שוועל

און שווײַגן.

טירן וועלן שטײַן אָפֿן ווי טײַסטערס בײַ גבֿירים פֿאַרן טויט;
וועלט וועט ווערן דין און דורכזיכטיק; איך נעם זען דורך דער
הויט

פֿון דעמער.

אַ שפּיל איז אַלץ, אַ שפּיל דאָס רויט און גרין
פֿון סעמאַפֿאָר אויף עק פֿון גאַס: מען מעג!
און אַלע מענטשן זײַנען מײַנע, ס׳איז מײַן פֿאַרמעג
איבער נאַכט.

190

Nightfall

The night will halt at my command
and my street won't stretch out as always;
the few trees that have something to say
will say it all at my threshold
and be silent.

Doors will stand open like the coin purses
of wealthy men before death;
the world will become thin and transparent;
I begin to see through the skin
of twilight.

Everything is a game, a play of red and green
from the semaphore at the end of the street:
The go-ahead signal! All the people are mine,
my holdings overnight.

זיך אָנכאַפֿן אין מאָצאַרטס אַ תּנועה
און אַזוי שוין בלײַבן הענגען.

איך דאַרף נישט גאָרנישט,
קיינער זאָל מיר גאָרנישט שענקען,
איך וויל נישט קיינעמס רײַכקייט אַרבן,

(ווי רײַך זײַנען בּיימער אין האַרבסט
און שטאַרבן אַלץ איינס,
און שטאַרבן ——)

פֿאַרפֿיר מיך נישט,
פּרוּוו מיך נישט פֿאַרפֿירן,
גאָסן פֿאַרגעסן זיך און טוען נאָך אַלץ
מיטן זומער שפּאַצירן.

נאָר איך בין נעבעך קלוג געוואָרן
און לייען אין די פֿאַלנדיקע בלעטער
הבל־הבלים,

כּאָטש אין מײַן לאַץ
איז נאָך אַלץ פֿאַרשטעקט,
ווי אַ בלום ——
אַ חלום.

Untitled

To hold on to Mozart's movement
and thus remain suspended.

I need nothing,
no one should give me charity,
I don't want to inherit anybody's riches,

(how rich the trees in autumn
and they die just the same
they die—)

do not lead me astray,
don't even try,
as streets forget and still
go on with summer.

Alas, I poor fool have become wiser
and read into the falling leaves
vanity of vanities,

although in my lapel
like a flower tucked away
there is still—a dream.

אַבֿי מיר זײַנען נישט אַליין...

דער אַמעריקאַנער דזשאַרדזש סמיט האָט אין *1961* געמאַכט די אַנטדעקונג אַז
אונטער מוזיקקלאַנגען וואַקסן די צמחים שנעלער.

אַבֿי מיר זײַנען נישט אַליין,
אַבֿי מיר האָבן אַ שותּף;
אפֿשר הערט אויך אַ שטיין?
וועלן מיר גליקלעך זײַן,
וועלן מיר גליקלעך זײַן,
ס'איז אַזוי פֿיל שווײַגן אין חלל
פֿון אונדז אַזש ביז גאָט,
נאָר אַ פֿויגל זינגט אַ מאָל שירה.
וואָס פֿאַר אַ ווערט האָט אַ פֿויגל
אַנטקעגן אַ שווײַגן פֿון גאָט?
וואָס פֿאַר אַ ווערט האָט אין קאָסמאָס
דאָס ביסל גערויש אין דער שטאָט?
און זע: עס הערן די צמחים
שווײַגנדיק רעדן זיי הויך,
אפֿשר הערט דער שטיין אויך?
וועלן מיר גליקלעך זײַן
וועלן מיר גליקלעך זײַן.

As Long as We Are Not Alone

*In 1961 the American George Smith discovered that musical sounds
promote the growth of plants.*

As long as we are not alone,
as long as we have a partner;
perhaps a stone also hears?
We shall rejoice,
we shall rejoice,
there is so much silence in space
between us and God,
only a bird sometimes sings.
What is the worth of a bird
compared to the silence of God?
What worth has the city's faint noise
in the cosmos?
And see: the plants hear
silently they speak aloud,
perhaps the stone also hears?
We shall rejoice,
we shall rejoice.

אונדזערע מאַמעס וועלן נישט זײַן בײַ אונדזערע טויטן...

סע וואַרט אַ וואַנט
אויף אונדזער לעצטער גרימאַסע
און אונדזערע מאַמעס
זײַנען אַזוי ווײַט פֿון אונדז,
אַ ים איז דאָ,
און זיי קענען נישט אַריבער.
אונדזערע מאַמעס וואָלטן אַ הייב טאָן
אַ וואָלקן־קראַצער,
אַ שטאָלענע בריק,
אַ וואָרף צו טאָן דעם טויט
וואָס קומט אונדז פֿאַרצוקן,
און מיר וועלן נאַריש רופֿן
לעצטע ווערטער
וואָס קיינער וועט נישט פֿאַרשטיין.

196

Our Mothers Will Not Be at Our Deaths

There waits a wall
for our last grimace
and our mothers are so far from us;
there is an ocean
and they cannot cross over.
Our mothers would lift
a sky-scraper
a steel bridge
to hurl at death
as it devours us,
and we call out
foolish last words
that no one will understand.

אָט אַזוי ...

אָט אַזוי, מען ווערט פּאַמעלעך אַלט,
ס׳ציט צו קעסטלעך בריוו און צו אַלבאָמען,
אַ פֿאָטאָגראַפֿיע בײַ אַ טײַך און בײַ אַ וואַלד
ווי אויף אַ בוים האָסט אויסגעקריצט אַ נאָמען.

ס׳איז אַ טרייסט אַן אַלטער גוטער בריוו
איז וויכטיק דען ווער ס׳האָט אים געשריבן?
דעם אַלטן בליִיכן אונטערשריפֿט
האָט די צײַט לאַנג שוין אָפּגעריבן.

נאָר גראָע בענקשאַפֿט דרימלט אין דער שטיל
און זיך אַליין באַגעגנסט גאָר אַן אַנדערן,
נאָך לאַנגן וועג צום ציל וואָס איז קיין ציל
און וואַנדערן ...

198

Thus

So it goes, one grows slowly old—
drawn to boxes of letters, to albums
with a photograph by a river and in a forest,
as though you'd carved your name on that tree.

A fine old letter is such a comfort—
really is it important who wrote it?
That faint, ancient signature
nearly erased by time.

Only grayed longing dozes in the stillness—
you meet yourself as quite another
wandering a lengthy way
to a goal that is no goal.

צי מיט מיר, צי אָן מיר,
וועלן טעג אויסגיין מיט אַ טויט, אַ האַרבן,
און באַריאַזקעס וועלן אַרומגיין און זוכן זייער פֿאַרלוירענע בענקשאַפֿט
און וויינען זוכנדיק.

און שטיינער וועלן זאָגן אַ סוף, אַן עק, פֿאַרפֿאַלן,
און שוויַיגן.
נאָר פֿייגל וועלן שטורעמען די הימלען און מאַכן סקאַנדאַלן
אויף צוויַיגן.

און גראָזן, וואָס האָבן זיך באַגענוגנט וואַקסן ביַי דער סאַמער ערד,
וועלן זאָגן: פֿאָטערל — טו מיט אונדז וואָס דו ווילסט,
נאָר נישט שטאַרבן.
ס׳וועלן זיי אויפֿאַסן די פֿערד,
נאָר די פֿערד וועלן אויך שטאַרבן.

און איך וועל זיַין אַ בלום דעמאָלט, צי עפּעס אַנדערש וואָס,
אין וועלכע די אַרבעטזאַמע ערד וועט מיַין געביין פֿאַרוואַנדלען.
די צייַט — די זשומענדיקע בין
וועט מיר אויסנאָגן דעם האָניק און די פֿאַרבן
פֿאַר דער אייביקייט,
איך וועל אַ בלום זיַין
און ווידער שטאַרבן.
און מענטשן וואָס וועלן דעמאָלט זיַין?
זיי וועלן מסתּמא טאָן דאָס און יענץ,
און אַז זיי וועלן נישט האָבן וואָס צו טאָן,
וועלן זיי זיך קוילען און שטאַרבן,
אָדער גלאַט אַזוי שטאַרבן —
אַ געשעפֿט צו שטאַרבן?

200

Untitled

With or without me
days will pass to their harsh death,
and birches will be transplanted and search for their lost longing
and weep as they're yearning.

And the rocks shall foretell: an end,
that's it, it's lost,
and say no more;
but birds will storm the sky and scandalize the branches.

And grasses satisfied to grow by the very earth
will plead: dear little father—do what you will
but don't let us die.
The horses will eat the blades of grass,
but the horses too will die.

I will be a flower then, or perhaps something else,
into which the industrious earth will have transformed my bones;
time—that buzzing bee
will draw out the honey and color
for eternity.
I will be a flower
and die again, and the people that will then be?
Perhaps they will do this and that,
and when they've nothing better to do,
they will slit each other's throat and die,
or just die—
it's no big deal to die.

חלומות

מײַן חלום גראָבט אַלץ טיף די שיכטן
פֿון מײַן קינדהײט, פּלאַסט נאָך פּלאַסט,
אַרײַן־אַרויס גייט גאַסט נאָך גאַסט
אין אונדזער הויז, אומגעריכט איז.

און געפֿאַרבט פֿון טאָג דאָס ליכט איז,
ווי מער געבראַקט מיט ניס, ווי ס׳פֿאַסט
פֿאַר חול־המועד, ווען אונדזער גאַס
מיט אַזאַ אָוונטליכט געדיכט איז.

עלנט צי איך פֿרי די דעק אָפּ
פֿון מײַן געלעגער, פֿרירעריק־קאַלט
קוקט אין שויב אַרײַן דער וואַלד.

איז אַזוי פֿיל טעג און וועג אָפּ?
אַזוי פֿיל וועג פֿון מיר צו מיר
ווי פֿון פּוילן קײן סיביר.

Siberia: Dreamsongs

My dream digs deep into the strata
of childhood, layer after layer:
out of our house go
guest after guest; everyone an unexpected player.
And the clear light of dawn is colored
by the day, when, like Khalemoyed mead
sprinkled with nuts,
our street is thick with such evening light.

Forlorn, I pull back the covers in early morning;
from where I've lain the freezing cold forest
looks through my window pane.

How many days and ways have passed—
as much distance from me to me
as from Poland to Siberia?

... און מעשׂיות הערן אין מלווה־מלכּה־נעכט,
און איך בין אַ שאָטן אין ווינקל אײַנגעהערט,
און מײַנע ייִדן זײַנען שטיקער הימל אויף דער ערד,
ייִדן ווי בײַ מערזערן אויפֿן בלעך.

און די לבֿנה גליצך פֿון צוויילגן ווי אַן עפּל מען ברעכט
און מיט קפֿיצת־הדרך פֿליִען פֿערד
אַהין ווו דער ווונדער איז באַשערט,
דער צדיק פֿירט מיטן שׂטן ערשט געפֿעכט.

פֿאַר וואָס געשעט קיין ווונדער, גאָט, נישט מער?
אַלע נעכט האָסטו געבריענגט אַהער,
פֿון גאַנצער וועלט און דאָ זיי אויסגעצויגן.

די לבֿנה זיך גנבֿעט אין אַ זײַט
און איז ווי קיין מאָל אַזוי ווײַט
און שעמט זיך צו קוקן אין די אויגן.

Siberia: Untitled

… and to hear wonder-stories at Melave Malke nights:
and I am a spellbound shadow in a corner,
and my Jews are pieces-of-heaven on the earth,
Jews being shaped by these tales
as if in a tin vessel pounded by a brass pestle.

And the moon, as though of the branches, is an apple you break,
and the horses jump the road, and fly
to that place where wonder is predestined—
now the saintly man is struggling with Satan.

God, why don't wonders happen anymore?
You have brought all the nights here
from the whole world, and from the first stretched them out.

The moon slips away;
it has never been so distant,
so shy of my eye.

אַגינסקיס פּאָלאָנעז אין סיביר

ביז פֿופֿציק גראַד די פֿראָסטיק־שטײַפֿע טעג,
װוּ װעסטו זיך אַהינטאָן, מײַן דינער, װײכער ניגון?
דאָ לאָזן זיך בעריאָזעס נישט פֿאַרװיגן,
זײ גליװערן מיט שנײ, פֿאַרשיט בײַם װעג.

מיט דײַן פּאָלאָנעז אין ברוסט װי אַ פֿאַרמעג,
און ראָדיאָ־קלאַנגען װאַרעמען אָן דעם שטח,
איך װעל אַרױס אַ זיגער פֿון געװעט איצט,
נאָך פֿאַרן קלאַנג דערגרייכן כ'װעל דעם ברעג.

בײַם ברעג אין האַרבסט, ס'פֿאַלן נאָך געלע בלעטער,
און אַ האָנט איז דאָ װאָס צײלט זיי איבער שפּעטער,
און יעדער בלאַט איז אַ ליבעבריװ אין טרױער.

מײַן קינדהייט בלאָנקעט דאָרט אױף טױקער פּאָליאַנע,
נישט פֿאַרשטײיענדיק, זי האָט טיף אַזױ פֿאַרשטאַנען
און בענקט, װי דו, בײַם פֿאַרמאַכטן טױער.

Siberia: Oginski's Polonaise in Siberia

Days frozen stiff, as low as fifty below;
where will you find a home, my thin soft melody?
Birch trees along the road are so rigid with snow
they can't let themselves be swayed to sleep.

Possessed within my breast by your Polonaise,
even this vastness is warmed by radio sounds;
now I can win the bet,
I can reach the camp's edge before the sound dissipates…

Beyond the boundary it is autumn; yellow leaves are still falling,
and later a hand will count them—
each leaf a sorrowful love letter.

My childhood loses itself in this glistening glade,
not grasping what it has so deeply understood,
and, like you, yearns at the locked Gate.

א תפילה פון א מענטשן אין שניי

ס׳איז הײַנט קיין בלוטפֿלעק נישטאָ אין שניי,
מ׳האָט קיינעם נישט געשאָסן, איז שניי און שניי.
אַרום דיר — שניי,
אין דיר — שניי,
ווײַס צו ווײַס.

אָ, באַהיט מיך, גאָט, פֿון די שנייִיִקע ווערטער:
מנא מנא תקל ופֿרסין.
פֿאַרן דאָרפֿיש פנים: שניי
פֿאַרן הימל וואָס האָט נישט ווו צו פֿאַלן
און פֿאַלט אין שניי,
פֿאַר טױערלעך צעװײגטע אין װינט
װאָס האָבן אַזױ פֿיל צו זאָגן
און זאָגן בלױז: שניי
פֿאַרן דאָרפֿיש פנים: שניי,
פֿאַר שחרית — שניי, מוסף — שניי, מעריבֿ — שניי,
פֿאַר מיזרח, מערבֿ, צפֿון, דרום — שניי,
אַ מענטש אין שניי,
אַ הונט אין שניי,
אַ פֿערד אין שניי.

דאָס טאָגל צײַלט װי אַ קינד ביז צװײ:
איינס — שניי,
צװײ — שניי,
שניי,
שניי.

Siberia: Prayer of a Man in Snow

Today there is no bloodstain
on the snow; no one was shot; there's just snow and snow
around you—snow
in you snow—white on white.

O protect me God, from snowy Words:
You have been weighed and found wanting.
God has numbered thy kingdom and finished it.
The face of the village: snow.
The sky that has nowhere to fall—
and sinks into snow.
The little gates swinging in the wind—
so much to say and only saying: snow.
For the village face—snow;
for morning prayers—snow, added prayers—snow, sunset
         prayers—snow,
for east, west, north, south—snow,
a man in snow
a dog in snow
a horse in snow.

This precious little day counts like a child
up to two:
one—snow
two—snow,
snow,
snow.

אויסגעחלומט שטיללעבן

א גלאָז טיי,
א שיינע, ריינע גלאָז טיי,
א היימישע, א שמעקנדיק-זיסע,
אין דין געשליפֿן גלאָז
אויף א שטילן טיש,
באַדעקט מיט ווײַס,

אין דער ליכטיקער שטוב,
א צײַטונג מיט נײַס,
א וואָזאָן ליידיקגיין,
גאָרנישט טאָן מאָרגן.
איך טרינק פֿאַמעלעך, פֿאַמעלעך
דעם כּוס
און רייכער
א געשמאַקן פּאַפּיראָס.

Siberia: Dreamed Up Still-Life

A glass of tea,
a lovely, clear glass of tea,
dear, sweet smelling,
in thinly polished glass
on a peaceful table,
covered with white,

in the sunlit house.
A newspaper with news,
a loafing plant,
nothing to do tomorrow.
Slowly, slowly I drink
the glass
and smoke
a delicious cigarette.

צו אַ פֿידלערין

אין שיר־השירים איז אַ האַלדז אַזאַ ווי דײַנע
פֿאַרגליכן צו דודס שלאַנקן טורעם.
נאָר צו וואָס פֿאַרגלײַכן מײַן קאָפּ נאָך אַלע פֿײַנען,
וואָס פֿאַלט אין דײַן אָרעם?

דײַן אָרעם וואָס אָפֿט אַזוי ניט־הי איז
בײַם אָנשטרענג פֿון שפּילן סעך־סעענעך.
ערשט ווען ס׳נעמען פֿינקלען דײַנע אויגן הינטער ווײַעס —
לאָז מיר דעם פֿלאַם פֿון דײַן שפּילן דערקענען.

דײַן אויג איז מיד ווי מײַן האַרץ.
און דײַנע ליפֿן שעפּטשען מיר אין אויער
אַזוי שטיל, אַזוי ווײַך, אַזוי צאַרט,
דאָס ניט־דערשפּילטע פֿון סעך־סעענס טרויער.

212

To a Woman Violinist

*Thy neck is like David's, a slim tower upon which
can hang a thousand ornamental shields.*
—Song of Songs

The violin hanging from your slim neck
ornaments it like one of David's shields,
but I cannot compare mine to the beauty
of yours around which your arms are arrayed,

arms that have become so other-worldly
with the challenge of playing Saint-Saen
that only your eyes burning beneath
their lashes reveal your inner fire,

your eyes as weary as my heart,
as your notes whisper in my ears
so quietly   so softly   so gently
I cannot shield myself from Saint-Saen's sadness.

דאָס בלייכע ייִנגעלע

דאָס לאַנד איז אַזוי ווײַט פֿון דיר,
בלויז אין צײַטונג גאָפֿן עס,
ווי ס'האָט דער הונגער אויסגעבלייכט
דאָס שוואַרצע ייִנגעלע פֿון ביאַפֿראַ.

הענטעלעך ווי שפּענדעלעך,
אַזאַ טרויער אין די אויגן איז:
און דאָס קעפּעלע — אַ קירבעסל,
איבערן שטענגעלע געבויגן איז.

דאָס ייִנגעלע דערמאָנט אַזוי
דאָס געטאָקינד, נישט הײַנט געדאַכט,
ווען דער וועלטס אויגן דאַן
געווען זענען צוגעמאַכט...

וועלן זיי ערשט כאָטש עפֿענען זיך
און אַ הילף געבן איצט?
עס איז דאָך באַלד שוין נישט כדאַי
אויף דער וועלט צו לעבן איצט!

214

The Sickly Little Boy

This country is so distant,
that only by his newspaper-captured gaze
does one see how hunger has sapped the energy
of this little black boy from Biafra

with hands as tiny as split twigs,
eyes of such sadness,
and a head bent like a small
squash's crooked stem.

This little boy haunts me
like a child in a Nazi ghetto. Never again
should the world's eyes be closed
like they were then!

Never again may we not be aware.
Never again may help not be given.
Never again may it be of no use
to live in this world!

כ׳גיי אַליין זיך נאָך

כ׳גיי אַליין זיך נאָך אויף ראַנד פֿון יאָרן,
ווי אַ פויער קליבט געבליבנס נאָכן שניט;
ס׳איז עפעס דאָ און דאָרט געבליבן
וואָס צום פֿולן שניט עס פֿעלט.

כ׳האָב עפעס דאָ און דאָרט געלאָזן,
ווי דער פויער לאָזט נאָכן ערשטן שניט,
און דווקא אָט נאָך דעם עס בענקט זיך, בענקט זיך,
ווי פֿון דײַן לעבן עס וואָלט געווען דער מיט.

216

I Follow Myself Alone

I follow myself alone on the rim of the years,
like a peasant gathering the gleanings after a harvest,
the chaff abandoned here and there,
that's missing from the full harvest.

I too have abandoned things here and there
like a peasant during the initial harvest,
and there is NOTHING other than that for which I long—
as though it were the very kernel of my life.

פֿיר מיך

פֿיר מיך אין פֿלעצער
ערגעץ־וווּ
וווּ עס זיצן
זייער גוטע
און זייער שלעכטע
מענטשן
נאָר ניט קיין
"גלאַטיקע"
מיט פֿנימער
ווי זייער
קאַליגראַפֿיש כּתֿבֿ,
מיר וועלן לאַכן
מיר וועלן וויינען
נאָר נישט
געגענצן.

Lead Me

Lead me back somehow to that place
where both
very good and very evil people
dwelt together
but there were no "smoothies"
like these slick double faced ones....

Lead me back to the pure era
of our ancient Assyrians font
where we might then laugh and cry together
and never become weary of each other.

שטילער

דאַרפסט אַלץ נאָך נישט קיין סך אויף צו ווערן פֿריידיק:
אַ קינד איז שטיל געשטאַנען און גענומען לויפֿן,
אַ דאַך פֿול מיט טויבן און פּלוצעם ווערט ער ליידיק,
אַ שטאַרקער רעגן וואָס פּויקט מיר אין די שויבן.

און ס׳איז דאָ אַ סך נאָך קלייניקייטן,
אַ ניגון איז אַוועק און דאָך געבליבן העַנגען,
עס מײדן זיך צוויי באַנאַנען ערגעץ אין דער וויַטן
פֿון אַ שויב עס פֿאַלט אַ בליק אויף לאַנג אים צו געדענקען.

Stillness

You still don't need very much to be happy;
a child stood still and started to run,
a roof full of doves and suddenly it's empty,
a strong rain on my windowpane beats like a drum.

And still more small things,
a melody left and still it lingered;
somewhere in the distance, two trains miss each other,
and from a pane there falls a glance long to remember.

אַ סך טרעפֿ פֿירן אַראָפֿ
צום ברייטן טײַך,
נאָר צום רויש פֿון די בײמער
איז אַ סך נעענטער...
בין איך רײַך
מיט גערויש אין גערוישן
און מיט גרין אין גרין,
וואָס ציט זיך אַהין, אַהין, אַהין,
ווו אומזין באַקומט אַ זין.

הייב נאָר אָן —
און איך וועל זיך דערמאָנען אַלץ
וואָס איז פֿאַרגאַנגען,
האָסט נאָר עפּעס פֿאַרשטאַנען
און אַ סך נישט פֿאַרשטאַנען,
נאָר דו גלייבסט מיר
ווי מײַן ליד
און ווי דעם פֿאַרנאַכט.

Untitled

Many stairs lead down
to the wide river,
but it is much closer
to the rustling of the trees.
I am rich with the faint sound
within sounds
and the green within green
that stretches beyond, beyond reality
to where the senseless make sense.

Just start
and I will recall all
that has passed;
you have understood a little,
and much you haven't;
but you believe me
as you believe my song
and the dusk.

שטריק בינדן מיך צו אָט דעם האָפֿן
ווּ שטיל זײַן
האָט זיך געלערנט אַפֿילו דער ווינט.
ווּ זעגלשיפֿלעך בלאָזן זיך אויף
אין דער וויַיט
ווי וויַיסע בערעלעך
און זיַינען ווי זיַידענע הערעלעך
פֿון אַ קינד.
דאָרט ווּ די ציַיט
קאָרטשעט זיך צונויף
אין אַ פֿעלדז,
און אין צוויי פֿאַרליבטע וואָס שטייען,
אין אַ בלימל,
און אין קינדעריש געוויין.

224

Untitled

Ropes bind me to this harbor
where even the wind
has learned to be still,
where sailboats in the distance
billow like white bear cubs,
and are like a child's silken hair.
There is where time contorts itself together
into a rock,
and into two lovers who stand,
into a little flower,
and into childish lament.

צום שטילן יום־טובֿ פֿון דײַן ליכטיקן געזיכט
איך זעץ מיך ווי אן אָרעמאַן צום טיש,
און פֿיל דאָס ווונדערלעך געמיש
פֿון פֿאַרב און קלאַנג, שאָטן און ליכט.

אָ שטער נישט מיט וואָרט, האָב מיך נישט ליב,
ס'איז פֿול מיט דיר אַפֿילו דײַן שפּילצײַג פֿון ליים,
פֿרעמדע שטאָט איז אָפֿגעריסן פֿון דײַן ריף
און איז אין דער היים.

Untitled

To the quiet holiday of your radiant face
I sit down, placed like a pauper at the table,
able to feel the marvelous mix
of color and sound, shadow and light.

Oh don't disturb it with words, with loving me,
even your toy of clay is full of you; you see
this alien city-seat has been ripped from your rib,
and I am at home.

ס׳איז נאָך דאָ זיך וווּ צו באַהאַלטן:
אין וואַלד פֿון דײַנע האָר פֿאַר רויש און פֿאַר די געוואַלדן
פֿאַר צו פֿיל זון וואָס פֿאַרבלענדט די אויגן
און דײַן שאָטן ווי אַ בוים איבערגעבויגן

און פֿאַר קינאה און פֿאַר שׂינאה פֿון שלעכטע
זייערע שמועסן אויף דײַן שווײַגן צו פֿאַרבײַטן
בײַמער ליבן זיך דאָך אויך אין זייער וואַקסן און זייער שטײַגן
און ליבנדיק און וואַקסנדיק זײ שווײַגן, שווײַגן.

Untitled

There is still a place to hide
in the forest of your hair—
from the noise and shouts,
from the harsh sun that blinds me,
from the jealous and hateful
words of the wicked.

There is still such a place to hide
in the forest of your hair
where even the half bent over trees
grow as they live and reach for me silently.

ס׳איז אַן אַנדער מין

אַליין זײַן,

אין אַ גרויסן

גרויסן שײנעם מויער

צווישן הונדערטער פנימער,

איין פנים,

איז פֿרעמד אַזוי

און נישט דערקלערט,

ווי די צווייטע זײַט

פֿון דער לבֿנה.

איך קען זיך קוים מאָלן אים:

פֿאַרבלאַסט זענען אַלע קאָנטורן,

נאָר ער גייט מיר נאָך

ווי אַ געוויין

אַ וויט, אַ וויט געוויין

ס׳איז אַוודאי איך אַליין

אין אַרומיקן געטומל.

Untitled

It's another kind of being

aloneness

even in a big beautiful building
amid hundreds of faces

a face

strange and unexplainable
like the other side of the moon's

pale contour

I can barely recognize
though it follows me everywhere

crying

faint, distant crying
certainly it is I

entrapped in turmoil.

זי איז נאָך אויך נישט די,
כאָטש דאָס בלויי פֿון איר אויג
דערמאָנט אינעם לעצטן גרין
פֿון בלעטער פֿאַרן וועלקן,
און מעג איר אויג זײַן געוועּנדט
שטענדיק אַהין, אַהין
ווו אַלע דײַנע חלומות צײיען,
און אָפּגעריסענע ווינטלעך
זײַנען אירע העֹנט,
ווינטלעך וואָס קושן דיך
פֿאַר נאַכט,
ווען אַלץ האָט דיך פֿאַרגעסן.

Untitled

She is also still not the one,
though the blue of her eye
recalls the last green
of leaves before they wilt,
and may her eye always be turned
yonder, yonder
where all your dreams pull you,
and her hands are
small wisps of wind,
gentle breezes that kiss you
at dusk
when all else has forgotten.

ער האָט זי נישט ליב...

ער האָט זי נישט ליב
וויינט זי, וויינט זי, אַ ביטער געוויין.
וויינען מיט אַלע וועלטן,
זיי האָט אויך עמעצער נישט ליב,
ס׳האָט עמעצער געטאָן פֿאַרפֿירן
ס׳העלפֿט נישט קיין צירן זיך און צירן.
זיי פֿאַרשטייען אים נישט,
און קענען זיך אַליין נישט פֿאַרשטיין.

234

He Doesn't Love Her...

He doesn't love her
she weeps, she weeps, a bitter lament;
all the world weeps with her;
somebody doesn't love them either,
somebody led them astray;
it won't help to dress things up, to assume airs;
people just can't understand him—
let alone themselves.

א ליד

אויסגעלײדיקט ווי פֿון אַ הויז וואָס מ׳ציט זיך אַרויס
איז אַלץ אין מיר, און איבערגעחזרט זענען אַלע ערטער
ווי ציטאַטן פֿיל מאָל געלײיענט, מער נישט וועקן.
אויף ווי לאַנג קענען קלעקן
[אַלטע?] קלוגע ווערטער?
ס׳איז האַרבסט,
און רעגן,
און לעצטער רויש
פֿון געבליבענע בלעטער
און אַזוי שטאַנדהאַפֿטיק
דאָס ביסל לאָמפּנשײן.
און אַזוי טרויעריק,
ווי ס׳וואָלט קיין פֿרילינג מער נישט זײן.

Song

I am as empty as a just vacated house—
and though I remember everything in it by heart
those memories and places are no longer possible.

How long can endearing words endure—
it's fall
it's rain-swept
it's the last rustle of remaining leaves,
the last glow of the lamp,
such sadness
as though spring were no longer conceivable.

לײדיק

דערווארט קײן סך פֿון מיר און כ׳בעט דיך: נישט באַדויער
פֿאַר מײנע קורצע בריוו וואָס האָבן נישט קײן פֿרײד;
דו בעטסט: אויב טרויער — טאָ זאָל זײַן טרויער
נאָר נישט קײן טרוקענע, סתּם פֿאָרמעלע רײד.

ביסט גערעכט פֿרײַנד נאָך לאַנגן דויער,
שטיטיש: כ׳בין פֿון דעם אויך ווײַט;
ווען דאָס האַרץ איז לײדיק אַפֿילו פֿאָרן טרויער
ווײסטו ערשט פֿון טרויער דעם באַטײַט.

238

Empty

I beg you not to expect much from me,
from my short, joyless letters, and don't regret anything.
You ask if it is sorrow I suffer from: Well then let it be called sorrow,
and only recognize that is an empty, cliché.

You're right, my friend, after long suffering
it so happens I too am at a remove from what was.
Look, it's when the heart is empty even before the mourning begins
that one can really know the meaning of sorrow.

איך וויל דיר אַ מאָל ברענגען
אין עק פֿון שטאָט
אין אַ פּלאַץ
וווּ זייער גוטע און
זייער שלעכטע מענטשן
זיצן
מיט פּנימער נישט
קלאָר ווי פּרעסקריפּשן־כתבֿ
נאָר נישט גראָ
און נישט מיט קאַליגראַפֿישע
סילועטן
ווי זייער כתבֿ

איך וויל טאַנצן מיט
מײַן געזונטן פֿוס
און וויינען מיט מײַן קראַנקן
און זיך וווּנדער
וואָס דו ביסט
נישט טרויעריק
נישט פֿריילעך
נאָר קאַלט
ווי דער יאַנואַר

Untitled

I will sometimes take you
to the edge of the city
to a place
where very good and
very evil people sit
with faces not even as readable
as unfathomable prescription script,
but not old or gray
and not with crippled silhouettes
like their handwriting.

And I will dance with
my healthy leg
but cry with my sick one
and wonder
that you are
not sad
not happy
but cold
like January.

דאָס רעקלאַמע־בילד

ס׳איז גאָר נישט וואָס דײַנע אויגן
שײַנען צו מיר אַרויס פֿון עפּעס אַ רעקלאַמע,
אין אַ נאַרישן זשורנאַל,
בײַ אַ פֿלאַש ווײַן,
מײַן פֿײַן
ווערט אַלץ אײַנס
טיפֿער און שענער.
מעג איך גאָרנישט וויסן וועגן דיר:
צי ביסט אַ מאַמע,
צי אַ געליבטע,
אָדער בלויז אַ מיידל,
וואָס לעבט פֿון רעקלאַמעס...
צו באַוווּנדערן בלויז דײַנע וווּנדערלעכע ליפּן,
בלויז אַ ביסל אָפֿן,
כּדי צו זען די שיינע ציין.
און די נאָז אַזוי אָנגעמאַסטן
און פֿײַן,
כ׳הייב אָן צו פֿאַרשטיין
פֿאַר וואָס גאָט האָט בײַ די דער שיינקייט
פֿון רעגנבויגן געשוווירן,
אַז ס׳זאָל קיין מבול מער נישט זײַן...

242

The Advertising Picture

It's not just that your eyes
shine out to me from a mere advertisement
in a silly magazine
near a bottle of wine,
it's that you make my anguish
all the more deep and beautiful.

I know nothing about you—
if you are a mother
or have a lover
or are just a girl
that lives off advertisements.

But when I admire your wonderful lips
open just enough
to reveal your beautiful teeth,
and your nose that fits just right
and is so refined—
I begin to understand
why God at the beauty
of the rainbow vowed
there would never be a flood again.

שפּיטאָל-רעפֿלעקסן

זיי קושן מיך, נאָר כ'גלייב זיי נישט...
נאָר איר האָב איך יאָ געגלייבט,
די נוירס, אַרום צוועלף בײַ נאַכט, בשעת זי
האָט זיך צעווײנט און מיך געקושט
זיצנדיק בײַם ראַנד
פֿון מײַן בעט
און ווען יעדער קעגנשטאַנד
רעדט
פֿאַר פֿײַער און פֿאַר וואַסער...

זי האָט עפּעס וועגן מיר געהערט,
און מיטגעליטן אַזוי ערלעך:
עס הענגט די שוועדד
איבער מײַן קאָפּ,
און ס'איז איר, ווי מיר,
אַזוי שווערלעך,
אַזוי שווערלעך...

אָ, מיטן נאַכט אין הויז פֿון טויט!
דער טויט איז שווערער דאָ ווי אין דרויסן,
ווען אַלץ וואָס נאָענט איז אַזוי ווײַט —
כ'נאַר זיך נישט, כ'ווייס גענוי,
וואָס דײַן קוש איז איצטער אויסן,
איך געטרויי, געטרויי, געטרויי
זײַן רירנדיקער מענטשלעכקייט,
וואָס דו קענסט זיך מער ווי מיט דײַן
שיינקייט גרויסן.

Hospital Reflections

They kiss me but I don't believe them—
but I did believe you, the nurse who
about midnight started to cry
and kissed me sitting at the edge
of my bed incessantly talking
about all kinds of topics.

She had heard about me
and empathized so honestly…
understanding the sword that
hangs so heavily over my head
hangs as heavily over hers…

Oh middle of the night in the house of death!
Death that is more difficult here than elsewhere
in places the nearness of death is more distant—
I don't deceive myself, I know exactly
the content of your kiss
and I trust, trust, trust
it is your humanity not your beauty
that moves you to this haughty compassion.

גאַנצער [—] און ריטפֿערע מוזיק,
בין איך אַלץ נאָך גרייט אָפּצושטיין ביי אַ פֿענצטער
אַ פֿיאַנאַ־גאַמע הערנדיק די קלענסטע
ווי צו צען יאָר, ביים יינגל, דאָס [שענסטע?] גליק.

דיין לעבן פֿאַרנייגט זיך שוין צום ענד
און דיין יעדער טראָט קען זיין דער לעצטער פֿון דיינע טריט
אַ פֿיאַנאָקלאַנג—און דיין געמיט
צו דיין קינדהייט איז צוריק געווענדעט

מיין גוטער פֿריינט געשטאָרבן אַ צייט צוריק
האָסט גאָרנישט אַנגעווויירן מיין גוטער פֿריינט
אַזוי איבערגעהזרט אַלט, די זון עס שיינט
ווי דעמאָלט אַזוי מיד אויך היינט

זי וואָלט זיך אָפּשטעלן און עמעץ טרינקט [—]
און געשעענישן וויקלען זיך באַנאַנד
און זוכן בלויז אין אַנדערן [—]
מיין פֿריינט ס'איז [—]

Untitled

Mature now in years and musical tastes,
I am still the ten year old
standing by a window listening
to a piano scale or a simple song—
transfixed by its hint of happiness.

My life is bending to its end
each step may be my last,
but the sound of a piano still
sends my spirit back to childhood.

Dear friend, dead for some time,
nothing is lost, dear friend
even the tired old sun remains standing,
still shining as it always did.

My age-old friend,
events collapse into each other,
the new seeks the old, but you have
lost nothing to the land of the dead.

הערנדיק באַך אין צווייען

מיר קענען זיך צו פיל —
קענען מיר שוויגן צוזאַמען,
באַך טראָגט זיך ווי אַ נס
פון שפילקאַסטן אין דער מאַשין.

פֿאָרגעס,
וווּהין מיר דאַרפֿן באמת פֿאָרן,
הער, הער די שפיל,
זי פֿירט אונדז וווּטער,
נישט אַהין ווו מיר דאַרפֿן גיין.

הער, הער, הער,
און ווער
דאָס וואָסט דו ווילסט זײַן:
נישט מאַמע, נישט ווײַב, נישט פֿרוי,
נאָר עפעס אין דער לופֿט
אַ גרויסער שמייכל צי אַ טרער.

לערן זיך, לערן זיך מיט אים גיין
אויף זײַטיקע, זײַטיקע וועגן
(דער הויפטוועג איז נישט פֿאַר אונדז,
לאָזן אַנדערע אויף אים גיין).
גייט דען נישט נאָך אַ געוויין
פון אַ פֿאַרגעסענעם בליק
וואָס מיר האָבן ווו געלאָזן
אויף אַ זײַטיקן וועג,
אויף אַ שטעג.
זע אים אַצינד,
ער איז נישט געגאַנגען פֿאַרלאָרן,
כאָטש ס'זענען אָנגעוואַקסן
אזוי פֿיל יאָרן
אויף אונדז.

On Both of Us Listening to Bach

We know one another too well
so we can be silent together
as Bach is wafted like a miracle
from the car radio.

Forget where we must really travel to
and listen, hear the playing that can
lead us farther and further than
our actual destination or where we've been.

Listen   listen   listen
and become what you want to be
not mother, not wife, not even just woman
but something floating in the air
as big as a smile or a tear....
that exists only in our dreams
or the mirror
or a mother's lullaby
over a crib...

Learn, teach yourself to travel with Bach
on these very very secondary roads;
since the main road is not for us,
let others walk it.

Doesn't the crying from a forgotten glance
that we've left somewhere on a side road
or some path still follow us?
Now can't you see it has not gone astray
even though so many years
have overgrown our way.

לאָז מיך נישט איבער אַליין

פֿאַר מיר צעשנײדט די נאַכט זיך
אויף שװאַרצע פֿיר שפּיגלען,
און פֿון דער װעלט גייט אויף אַ געװיין
װי פֿון קינדער פֿאַרלאָזטע אין װיגלען,
לאָז מיך נישט איבער אַליין...

ס׳איז אַלץ אַװעק פֿון מיר
װי פֿון אַן אָרעמאַן אַנטלויפֿט
אַ קרובֿ װאָס איז רײַך:
ס׳אַנטלויפֿט פֿון מיר דער װאַלד,
ס׳אַנטלויפֿט דער טײַך.
און דער ניגון איז שײן,
נאָר ער װיל אויך שלאָפֿן גיין —
לאָז מיך נישט איבער אַליין...

ס׳האָט װער מיר געמאַכט
פֿאַרן װעכטער פֿון דער נאַכט,
און שװער איז מיר איר שטח אַרומצוקריגזן,
װיי פֿון טאָג צעקרישלט זיך װי גלאָז
און פֿאַרשטעכט זיך אין מײַנע שפּרײזן.
שטילקייט, שטילקייט, שטילקייט
שװערט אַראָפּ װי אַ שטיין —
לאָז מיך נישט איבער אַליין...

250

Don't Leave Me Alone

For me night cuts itself
into four black mirrors
and a lament arises from the world
as from a child abandoned in a crib—
don't leave me alone...

For me everything has departed
like a rich relative runs from a pauper:
The forest grows from me.
The river flows away
and melody is lovely
but it too ceases—
don't leave me alone...

Someone has made me
the watchman of the night,
but it's hard to walk that distance
when hurts of the day crumble like glass
splinters embedding at each step.
Silence silence silence
comes down heavy as a stone—
don't leave me alone...

1956

"Before You Extinguish Me": The Yiddish for "extinguish me" could also be translated "snuff me out," as with a flickering candle.

"The End of the Story": Emiot was familiar with the Indian writer Rabindranath Tagore, who won the Nobel Prize in 1913. "I bury myself in my arms and dream that my paper boats float on and on under the midnight stars." The poem is found in multiple books with different titles.

Simkhes-Toyre is the holiday devoted to celebrating the Torah.

"Arizona Desert": "Grandmother," Yiddish word is Bubbe.

Khumesh, Pentateuch, Torah, the five Books of Moses.

Allegedly the Jews could have gone quickly to Canaan, but God punished Moses who wanted to go back to Egypt, and was taken away on the threshold of entry.

Special Yiddish prayers for women called The Şena Rena; literally the words mean, "go out and see." Women did not traditionally learn Hebrew.

It is the Yiddish tradition to ceremonially unveil a gravestone one year after death.

At Bar Mitzvah one accepts responsibility of the Torah and the Father says, "You are responsible now, not I, for your actions and way of life."

Bialik poem: Those who died in the desert were to arise as a new generation. But Joshua said, "Those who spurn me shall not see the promised land."

"Untitled" ("With or without me..."): Emiot is likely to have read Herman Hesse's poem "After Deaths" in the original German. See translation by James Wright in *Poems*, by Herman Hesse, (Farrar, Strauss and Giroux, 1970).

"Dreamsongs" (My dream digs deep): Khalemoyed: the four days between the first two and last two days of Pesach, or Passover.

"Untitled" ("...and to hear wonder-stories..."): "Melave Malke": Literally, to escort the Queen, a Chasidic ceremony at the end of Sabbath to escort the spirit of Sabbath out the door.

"Oginski's Polonaise in Siberia": Michal Kleofas Oginski, 1765-1833, was (and still is) a popular Polish composer.

"Prayer of a Man in Snow": "God has numbered thy kingdom and finished it": Literally an acrostic from the Book of Daniel.

"To a Woman Violinist": The lines from Song of Songs are based on the translation in The New American Standard Bible, 1995.

"The Sickly Little Boy": Original publication in *Unsere Zeit* (Our Time), 1976.

"I Follow Myself Alone": Original publication in *The Jewish Eagle,* 1975.

"Lead Me": The poem refers to the history of Hebrew calligraphy, which has had many historically and religiously distinct and significant fonts. For some Jews, the earliest is the most sacred.

"Untitled" ("Many stairs lead down..."): "but you believe me"—Saul Tchernikovsky, Hebrew poet: from the poem, "Credo," "Laugh at all my dreams my dearest, / laugh and I repeat anew, / that I still believe in mankind, / and the spirit in him born."

"Untitled" ("To the quiet holiday of your radiant face..."): "Toy of clay" refers to Adam being made of clay and to the Golem, which in Jewish folklore is an unfinished being made of clay. A kind of reverse play on the Adam and Eve story.

"Untitled" ("She is also still not the one..."): "Pull you": Mignon, opera by Thomas, text by Goethe: "Do you know the land where the citroen blossoms / blooms there, there, my dreams pull me there."

"The Advertising Picture": Original publication in *Unsere Zeit*, 1974.

"Hospital Reflections": Original publication in *Tsukunft (The Future)*, 1975. In general, and particularly in this poem, Emiot was inspired by the work of the distinguished Yiddish writer Yisroel Shtern, who probably died in the Warsaw Ghetto. See Australian Centre for Study of Jewish Civilization, Monash University, 2006, and the recent book edited by Andrew Firestone, *Yisroel Shtern: Collected Poems Warsaw 1919-1939*, (Kadimah, Paris, 2014).

"On Both of Us Listening to Bach": There are four almost illegible versions of this poem. It is largely the order of the stanzas that is different in each, with only a few lines omitted in one. It was likely written in the early 1970s.

Translator's Addendum

ISRAEL EMIOT WAS NOT MURDERED by Stalin subsequent to the trials in 1952, now commemorated as *The Night of the Murdered Poets*. However, he, and others, were incarcerated in Gulags (Soviet labor camps/prisons, existing 1934-1955), and suppressed as writers, or had earlier been enslaved by the Nazi war machine, or even in some cases had been co-opted by Soviet ideology.

In the last fifty years or so, world-wide awareness of Soviet duplicity with regard to Jews who voluntarily or otherwise fled into the Soviet Union, beginning in the 1930s, has increased and continued. A fortunate corollary of this new-found awareness has been the growing rescue, translation, and appreciation of the poetry and other literature by these ill-fated writers. (This era also included the murder of beloved actor and film director Solomon Michoels, the suppression/torture/incarceration of various other artists and scientists, and the so-called Jewish Doctor's Plot. It has continued into the present decades with the persecution and/or suppression of Soviet writers and other personages—often of Jewish origin.)

Therefore, despite the deliberate emphasis by this translator on the literary aspects of Emiot's life and oeuvre, it is imperative to provide a brief overview of the politics of the era. A formidable body of historical research, reportage, and sleuthing has resulted in currently available books and articles by Joseph Sherman, Joshua Rubenstein, Daniel Shneer, Gennady Estraikh, Nathan Englander and many others. I am indebted to their endeavors, as well as personal conversations with survivors of those times, including the writer Joseph Kerler.

Initially, Stalin and his regime supported the establishment of the Moscow State Yiddish Theatre (GOSET), and promoted the writing of Peretz Markish, Moyshe, Kulbak, Hillel Halkin, Itsak Feffer, Dovid Bergelson, Leib Kvitko, David Hofshteyn, etc. Stalin established Birobidzhan in 1928 as an autonomous Soviet-Jewish Republic with Yiddish as its official language in schools, periodicals and street names. Overall the goal was to transform eastern European Jewry into socialist-communists-Marxists as a condition of their survival in the USSR, and thereby use Jews to bolster the post-Revolutionary period in Russia. However, by 1938 Russian had been made the official language. By the time of the duplicitous Molotov-Ribbentrop Pact in 1939, officialdom of the Soviet government had already been purged of Jews; Litvinov was replaced by Molotov, for example, though even he had a Jewish wife.

But with the onslaught of WWII, the Soviets again relented and established the JAFC, the Joint/Jewish Anti-Fascist Committee. The Yiddish paper *Eynikeyt (Unity)* had begun to flourish and *Der Emes (Truth)* became an official Russian-Yiddish publisher. Emiot published his book *Lider* in 1940 with Emes, and was later sent from Moscow by the JAFC to Birobidzhan as a journalist. Thus he did not remain in Khazhkstan in a desperate work battalion as a war-refugee.

However, Stalin had secretly already begun another anti-Jewish and anti-Semitic thrust, arguing for a pure Russian art, or else. Yet emissaries were sent to the USA to garner support for the Russian war effort and a second front. One of those sent was later alleged to be a double agent. And various left-wing Americans, sympathetic to Jewish culture, were invited to the USSR, such as Paul Robeson. After World War II, matters went drastically downhill for the Jews in Russia. Only after Khrushchev's famous speech in 1956 distancing himself from Stalin, did Jewish life in the USSR improve somewhat. Through the next several presidencies, little changed. However, during Perestroika under Gorbachev, the situation became more hopeful. Currently, in the Putin era, Jewish rights are being compromised once again. Emiot was released from the Gulag in 1957. Thus it can truly be said that Jewish life in the USSR had become a unique continuation of sorts of Hitler's Holocaust.

Nevertheless, this dreadful saga, much abbreviated herein, had its silver lining for Yiddish/Jewish literature: Because the Jewish intellectuals under discussion did in fact move away or out to some degree from their traditional writing genres, forms, and ways of being, they were able eventually to transcend their shtetl life and join world literature on their very own Jewish, cultural terms. Factors that made this possible included contact with enlightened or secular ideology, life in bigger city centers, the force of different political events world-wide, feminism, technology, the sheer displacement and diasporic emigration, and of course the Holocaust. They did it with varying degrees of abandonment or enrichment. Some better than others. And always with enormous personal cost.

It is evident in Emiot's writing both in Europe and the United States, that he was one of those who were able to maintain and sustain their Jewish roots while simultaneously growing in a worldly literary life. Perhaps the earliest examples of this are his referencing Polish icons Slowaki and Oginski in his Siberia poems, and his admiration for Rilke. Thus, *The Night of the Murdered Poets* is cause for great mourning, but not total despair about Yiddish literature. Emiot and this book are a case in point.

Books by Israel Emiot

In Yiddish:

Alone with Oneself, 1932, Ostrov, Poland, poetry.

Drop in the Ocean, 1935, Mnora, Warsaw, Poland, poetry.

At My Side, 1936, Krakow/Lodz, Poland, poetry.

Over Partitions, 1936, Warsaw, Poland, poetry. Unobtainable.

Poems, 1940, Moscow, USSR, poetry.

Rising, 1947, Birobidzhan, poetry.

Yearning, 1957, Warsaw, Poland, poetry

In Melody Absorbed, 1961, Rochester, N.Y., prose and poetry.

Covered Mirrors, 1962, Buenos Aires, Argentina, prose and poetry.

In Middle Years, 1963, Rochester, N.Y., prose and poetry.

Before You Extinguish Me, 1966, Rochester, N.Y., poetry.

For the Sake of Ten, 1969, Rochester, N.Y., prose and poetry.

In English:

My Yesterdays, 1973, Rochester, volunteer anthology by Jewish Community
      Federation, prose and poetry.

Life in a Mirror, 1976, Ibid.

The Birobidzhan Affair, 1981, Philadelphia, Jewish Publication Society of
      America, prose, translator Max Rosenfeld.

Siberia, 1991, Rochester, NY, State Street Press, poetry, bilingual. Translated
      by Leah Zazulyer.

Acknowledgements

Grateful acknowledgement is made to the editors and publishers of the following journals and publishing houses where the following poems appeared originally:

"Let's Detain the Summer," 1987, *Der Pakentreger*, National Yiddish Book Center, H. Winson Prize. And also in *Beacons* #8, 9, 2002, SUNY Dept. of English, Plattsburgh, NY; also "Before You Extinguish Me," and "Our Mothers Will Not Be at Our Deaths."

"As Long as We're Not Alone," 1996, *Visions International*, #52. And also 2011, Poetry Art Walk, Rochester, NY.

"My God I Believe in You So Much," "A Prayer in Nineteen Forty-Three," "Prayer of a Man in Snow," and "With and Without Me," 1991, *Seneca Review*, Vol. XXI.

"Umschlagplatz," 2002, *In Posse Review*, Berkeley, CA.

"Hour of Sadness" and "As Long as We're Not Alone," 2004, *Passports*, V. Smith, McKinney, TX.

"Prayer of a Man in Snow," "Untitled," and "A Prayer in Nineteen Forty-Three," 2009, *Poetry International* #13, 14, San Diego, CA.

"Los Angeles," "Hour of Sadness," and "End of Story," 2009, *Harper's Ferry Review*; "Los Angeles," 2010, California Institute for Yiddish Culture, Hon. Mention.

"Dreamsongs," "Melave Malke," "Oginski's Polonaise," "Prayer of a Man in Snow," and "Dreamed-Up Still Life," in *Siberia*, published by State Street Press, 1991.

Special Acknowledgements

David T. Smith and Laura Silkes, for technical and editorial assistance.

James Bearden, for volunteering to scan the Yiddish by hand, and so much more.

Arun Viswanath, for Yiddish typography, spelling modernization, proofreading, and even more subtle refinements—while at the same time teaching English on a Fulbright in India.

Steven Huff, publisher, editor, writer, for enthusiasm, talent, patience and wisdom.

Phil Memmer, for English typography, and design of the text and cover.

Richard Beale for permission to reproduce his artwork, *In my joy even the stars come to visit* in the cover design.

About the Translator

Leah Zazulyer writes poetry and prose, translates Yiddish poetry, and is a retired special education teacher, consultant, school psychologist, and mediator. Originally schooled in comparative literature, she has long been interested in issues of language as it relates to culture, in "the geography of the imagination," and the "narrative of self." She lives in Rochester, New York, but grew up in a bilingual family in California that emigrated from Belarus. She has studied Yiddish as an adult privately in Rochester, and in summer programs at Oxford and Cambridge Universities.

She has received grants from the Constance Saltonstall Arts Foundation, the New York State Council on the Arts, the New York State Foundation on the Arts, and the Winston Translation Award from the Yiddish Book Center.

Her publications include selections in a variety of journals, magazines and anthologies, plus two poetry chapbooks: *The World Is a Wedding* and *Round Trip Year*; and also a full-length poetry book *Songs the Zazulya Sang*, and *Siberia*, a bilingual book of translations by Israel Emiot about his incarceration in a Soviet Gulag.

Recent collaborations include a Georgia O'Keefe word/art museum event, an artist/poet project with Kristin Malone, and a poem/word art project with Gail Vick that was the 2008 Caldecott purchase by the Newberry Library.

Current projects include work on a play, new poetry collections, more translations, and a completed series of poetic monologues based on interviews with Holocaust survivors in several cities.

She met Israel Emiot in literary circles in Rochester, but did not begin translating him until after his death. She is especially pleased to be a part of the current worldwide renewal of interest and translation of Yiddish literature.

More Poetry from Tiger Bark Press